ORTHODOX CHRISTIAN
SOCIAL THOUGHT

Creation and the Heart of Man

**An Orthodox Christian
Perspective on Environmentalism**

Fr. Michael Butler

Andrew P. Morriss

Edited by Dylan Pahman

ACTONINSTITUTE

Orthodox Christian Social Thought Series, Number 1

© 2013 by Acton Institute

Acton Institute
for the Study of Religion and Liberty

Cover image: Isaac Levitan (1860–1900). Above the Eternal Tranquility. Moscow, Plyos. 1894.
Source: Public domain. Wikimedia Commons.

ISBN: 978-1-938948-67-1

ACTONINSTITUTE

98 E. Fulton
Grand Rapids, Michigan 49503
Phone: 616.454.3080
Fax: 616.454.9454
www.acton.org

Cover design by Peter Ho
Copy edited by Jan M. Ortiz
Interior composition by Judy Schafer

Printed in the United States of America

Contents

At the center of the universe beats the heart of man.

—Vladimir Lossky

Man can turn earth into paradise only if he carries paradise within himself.

—Bases of the Social Concept
of the Russian Orthodox Church

1 Introduction

There is a way of living in the world that promotes and sustains right relationships between God and man, between man and his neighbor, and between man and the rest of the created order.[1] The Orthodox Church teaches this way, and its teaching offers insights into ways we might address the environmental issues that confront us today. This teaching can be found in the classical texts of Christian tradition, as well as in recent and contemporary Orthodox writers. We will be drawing heavily on their work throughout these pages.[2]

---

[1] Our consideration of the relationship between Orthodox theology and environmentalism began at an Environmental Stewardship Conference for Religious Leaders, "Breakthrough: Ethics, Economics and the Environment" (sponsored by FREE, the Foundation for Research on Economics and the Environment, Bozeman, MT, September 8–12, 2008), and we gratefully acknowledge their inspiration. Similarly, the Acton Institute patiently supported the lengthy gestation of this project. William Brewbaker and Dylan Pahman provided invaluable comments. All remaining errors, of course, are our responsibility.

[2] It will be necessary to emphasize some aspects of Orthodox thought for the sake of our thesis, those that support our interest in environmentalism, and leave other aspects aside, so readers should not expect comprehensive expositions of Orthodox teaching or

The Orthodox voice has not been widely heard on environmental issues. In the 1890s, the Russian philosopher Vladimir Solovyov anticipated modern concerns for the environment when he put forward a new consideration that "has never yet been insisted upon," namely "the duties of man as an economic agent toward material nature itself, which he is called upon to cultivate." Solovyov claimed that "without loving nature for its own sake it is impossible to organize material life in a moral way," and "the ideal is to cultivate the earth, to minister to it, so that it might be renewed and regenerated."[3] However, his considerations on the treatment of material nature were not developed further. In our own day, the first major declaration by an Orthodox Christian on environmental concerns was issued on September 1, 1989. The *Message on the Day of Prayer for Creation*, by the Ecumenical Patriarch, Demetrios I of Constantinople, decried "the merciless trampling down and destruction of the natural environment which is caused by human beings, with extremely dangerous consequences for the very survival of the natural world created by God." It went on to declare, "the first day of September of each year to be the day of the protection of the environment, a day on which, on the occasion of … the first day of the ecclesiastical year, prayers and supplications are [to be] offered … for all creation."[4] The next year, an important document, *An Orthodox Statement on*

---

balanced considerations of it in what follows. Moreover, we note that the Fathers did not use gender-neutral language and so here we caution that our references to *man* should be seen as inclusive references to both men and women.

[3] Vladimir Solovyov, *The Justification of the Good: An Essay in Moral Philosophy*, trans. Nathalie A. Duddington, ed. and annot. Boris Jakim (Grand Rapids: Eerdmans, 2005), 299–300.

[4] The English text can be found at http://www.goarch.org/ourfaith/ourfaith8052.

the Environmental Crisis, was drawn up under the auspices of the Ecumenical Patriarchate by a group of theologians and environmentalists in Ormylia, Greece.[5] Since then, Orthodox writing on environmental issues has continued to grow.[6] In addition to statements and conferences on environmental topics, the Orthodox world has seen a blossoming of "hundreds of local initiatives and projects ranging from soil reclamation projects in Russia to tree planting initiatives in Romania to

---

[5]   Available at http://www.arcworld.org/faiths.asp?pageID=121.

[6]   Increasing numbers of Orthodox writers are engaging with the issues. The most prominent Orthodox Christian addressing environmental issues today is Ecumenical Patriarch Bartholomew I of Constantinople (the successor of Demetrios I), who has come to be known as the "Green Patriarch" because of his sustained interest in and promotion of environmental causes internationally. Particularly notable are the patriarch's annual *Message on the Day of Prayer for Creation* and the ecological symposia *Religion, Science and the Environment* on water pollution, for example, on the Aegean Sea (1995), the Black Sea (1997), the Danube River (1999), the Adriatic Sea (2002), the Baltic Sea (2003), the Amazon River (2006), the Arctic Sea (2007), and the Mississippi River (2009). For a summary of the Patriarch's activities, see Philip Abrahamson, "The Green Patriarch: Orthodox Environmental Participation," *Journal of Faith and Science Exchange* 6 (2010), http://open.bu.edu/xmlui/handle/2144/4020, article currently unavailable. The Russian Orthodox church included a statement on "The Church and Ecological Problems" in its important document, the *Bases of the Social Concept of the Russian Orthodox Church*, issued in 2000, available in English at http://www.3saints.com/ustav_mp_russ_english.html, and more recently, on February 5, 2013, the Holy Synod of Bishops issued a document, *The Position of the Russian Orthodox Church on the Issue of Ecology*, http://www.synod.com/synod/eng2013/20130205_ensobordocument.html. Other notable Orthodox writers and their more accessible works are cited passim.

wildlife preservation programmes in the Greek islands and to forest preservation on the Holy Mountain."[7]

Despite its promotion in the highest circles of the Orthodox Church, we confess our disappointment with much of the Orthodox writing on the environment. In light of the capture of environmental issues by the left-of-center portion of the political spectrum, we are not surprised that many Orthodox writers concerned with environmental degradation display a deep left bias in their writing. We are particularly disappointed, however, to see the following five issues.

First, appeals to the Orthodox Tradition and left/liberal policy recommendations that merely run parallel to each other, rather than deriving policy prescriptions clearly from Orthodox theological principles, as if abandoning Styrofoam cups at the parish coffee hour or encouraging population control self-evidently followed from the Tradition.[8]

---

[7] Alexander Belopopsky, *Introduction to Christian Environmental Initiatives*, http://www.goarch.org/ourfaith/ourfaith8051.

[8] See Vincent Rossi, "Styrofoam and Saint Isaac the Syrian: Toward an Orthodox Environmental Ethic," http://www.orth-transfiguration.org/styrofoam-and-saint-isaac-the-syrian/. For a similar treatment of visiting thrift and second hand stores, buying local, and public transportation, see Mandy Culbreath-Frazier, "Practical Suggestions for Environmental Stewardship," from the Orthodox Church in America's Department of Youth, Young Adult and Campus Ministries, http://ocawonder.com/2010/09/30/practical-suggestions-for-enviromental-stewardship/; and also Aidan Hart, "The Pain of the Earth: A Cry for Help," talk given in Minsk, Belarus, May 29, 2001, at the European Council of Churches' Christian Environmental Network Conference, 12. On population control, see Elizabeth Theokritoff, "A Eucharistic and Ascetic Ethos: Orthodox Christianity and the Environment," http://www.shapworkingparty.org.uk/journals/articles_0809/theokritoff, and Elizabeth Theokritoff, *Living in God's Creation: Orthodox Perspectives*

Second, the subordination of the Tradition to preexisting political or environmental agenda; for example, the tendency to minimize inconvenient truths, such as the centrality of mankind and his role in creation.[9] As Christians we cannot agree with American environmentalist and wilderness advocate John Muir (d. 1914), who said that the idea that the world was made for man is a "presumption not supported by all the facts."[10] As Christians, we know why the world was created and why it was entrusted to our care.

Third, the all-too-common tendency (not limited to the Orthodox) to focus exclusively on the negative aspects of Western society without acknowledging the benefits that accrue from it. For example, the *Bases of the Social Concept of the Russian Orthodox Church*, a significant document from the Russian church that addresses many contemporary social issues, begins its consideration of *The Church and Ecological Problems*, with a catalog of environmental woes. It goes on to say, "All this happens against the background of an unprecedented and unjustified growth of public consumption in highly developed countries, where the search for wealth and luxury has become

---

on Ecology (Crestwood, NY: St. Vladimir's Seminary Press, 2009), 257–58.

[9] See, for example, John Chryssavgis, "The World of the Icon and Creation: An Orthodox Perspective on Ecology and Pneumatology," in *Christianity and Ecology: Seeking the Well-Being of Earth and Humans*, ed. Dieter T. Hessel and Rosemary Radford Ruether (Cambridge, MA: Harvard University Center for the Study of World Religions Publications, 2000), especially the conclusion, 93.

[10] John Muir, *A Thousand Mile Walk to the Gulf*, ed. William F. Bade (Boston & New York: Houghton Mifflin, 1916), 136.

a norm of life."[11] Leaving aside the dubious claim that wealth and luxury are the engines of Western life, the *Bases* does not acknowledge that "highly developed countries" are among the cleanest, least polluting, and most energy-efficient societies in the world, nor does it draw on the Russian church's experience with the Soviet-era despoliation of the Russian environment;[12] or that effective measures addressing the environment may appear to be luxury goods outside of developed countries with enough wealth to give attention to environmental concerns, as demonstrated by the "environmental Kuznets curve";[13] or that Western technology has fueled the recent advances in pollution control,[14] food production,[15] and energy efficiency.[16] Yes, there are problems to be addressed, but credit should be given where credit is due.

---

[11] *Bases of the Social Concept of the Russian Orthodox Church*, 13.1.2, cited hereafter as *Bases of the Social Concept.*

[12] See Philip Rust Pryde, *Environmental Management in the Soviet Union* (Cambridge: University Press, 1991); Murray Feshbach and Alfred Friendly, Jr., *Ecocide in the USSR: Health and Nature Under Siege* (New York: Basic Books, 1992); Murray Feshbach, *Ecological Disaster: Cleaning Up the Hidden Legacy of the Soviet Regime: A Twentieth Century Fund Report* (Washington, DC: Brookings Institution, 1994).

[13] See Bruce Yandle, Madhusudan Bhattarai, and Maya Vijayaraghavan, *Environmental Kuznets Curves: A Review of Findings, Methods, and Policy Implications*, PERC Research Study 02-1 (April 2004), http://perc.org/articles/environmental-kuznets-curves.

[14] See, for example, Andrew Morriss, William T. Bogart, Roger E. Meiners, and Andrew Dorchak, *The False Promise of Green Energy* (Washington, DC: Cato Institute, 2011), 34, 159, and 213–14.

[15] Morriss et al., *False Promise*, 117, 154.

[16] Morriss et al., *False Promise*, 35–45.

Fourth, policy recommendations that take little or no account of economic reality. Here, we can cite Patriarch Bartholomew's *Message on the Nuclear Explosion at Fukushima*, issued on March 14, 2011, a scant three days after the earthquake and tsunami that devastated Japan (and several days before the Patriarch's message of sympathy to the Japanese people). The Patriarch wrote,

> With all due respect to the science and technology of nuclear energy and for the sake of the survival of the human race, we counter-propose the safer green forms of energy, which both moderately preserve our natural resources and mindfully serve our human needs.
>
> Our Creator granted us the gifts of the sun, wind, water and ocean, all of which may safely *and sufficiently* [emphasis added] provide energy. Ecologically-friendly science and technology has discovered ways and means of producing sustainable forms of energy for our ecosystem. Therefore, we ask: Why do we persist in adopting such dangerous sources of energy?[17]

Why indeed, if sun, wind, water, and ocean can *sufficiently* provide our energy needs? Of course, the answer is that they cannot.[18] They cannot for both technological and economic reasons. The sun shines only part of each day, the wind does not blow continuously, and tidal energy generation is in its infancy. The costs of these technologies are currently dramatically higher than conventional energy sources such as natural

---

[17] See http://www.patriarchate.org/documents/fukushima. Because the condolences of the Patriarchate to the Japanese people were not issued until ten days after the Japanese disasters and seven days after the "Message on the Nuclear Explosion," one cannot help questioning the timing of the Fukushima statement.

[18] See Morriss et al., *False Promise*.

gas, coal, and hydroelectric power. Wind turbines, solar panels, and tidal energy stations have serious environmental impacts of their own, including the need for massive transmission infrastructure that itself damages the environment. The problem faced by human societies, therefore, is one of making choices among imperfect alternatives, not a simplistic choice between "clean" and "dirty" energy sources. Further, our Creator also granted us energy stored in coal, oil, and natural gas, as well as embedding it within the bonds of matter, enabling us to meet our needs by responsibly using those sources of energy as well. Given the strong correlation between human well-being and electricity use, and our mandate to care for the poor, is it more important to raise energy costs by shifting to new "green" technologies or to provide electricity to the world's poor who lack access to power? Should getting cheap energy to the 412 million people in India (equivalent to the combined populations of Britain, Italy, and the United States) who lack any access to power be a higher priority than shuttering existing nuclear plants, as Germany is doing? Should providing natural gas to the 668 million Indians (equivalent to the populations of Britain, France, Germany, Italy, Japan, and the United States) who cook with dung or wood (a practice that is particularly damaging to the health of women and small children), be a higher priority than developing solar energy for Americans and Europeans? Is giving the 917 million Indians lacking refrigeration (equivalent to the entire population of the Western hemisphere) access to the electricity that would make that available more important than government subsidies for wind energy in rich countries?

Fifth, ignorance of modern economics. We do not follow certain teachings of the Fathers when later theological insight showed that they were in error,[19] nor do we follow the Fathers

---

[19] St. Gregory of Nyssa's (d. 395) teaching on universal salvation comes to mind.

when they express the faulty scientific or medical thought of their day.[20] Similarly, we need to be careful when the Fathers speak of economic matters. There is something to be learned, to be sure, in citing St. John Chrysostom (d. 407), that man is a "housekeeper" entrusted with the riches of the earth, and that these riches, "the air, sun, water, land, heaven, sea, light, and stars" are "divided among all in equal measure as if among brothers."[21] Failure to recognize that he is working in the context of a Malthusian economy where the ancient and medieval view of zero-sum economics prevailed can lead us to misapply St. John's words in the contemporary world in which much of humanity has thankfully escaped the Malthusian trap and entered into a positive-sum economy.[22] Indeed, a significant challenge for Orthodox (and Christian) thought is to avoid an outlook colored by envy and focused on distribution but rather to find ways to bring the insights of the Fathers and the teachings

---

[20] As, for example, St. John of Damascus (d. 749) does in his chapters on the natural world in book 2 of his *Exact Exposition on the Orthodox Faith* or St. Gregory Palamas (d. 1359) in his "Topics of Natural and Theological Science" found in the *Philokalia*.

[21] Cited in the *Bases of the Social Concept*, 13.2.

[22] On the escape from the Malthusian trap, see Deidre McCloskey, *Bourgeois Dignity* (University of Chicago Press, 2011). Regrettably, Patriarch Bartholomew I of Constantinople has misapplied St. John's words: "Not to share our own wealth with the poor is theft from the poor and deprivation of their means of life; we do not possess our own wealth but theirs, as a holy Father of the Church reminds us," in "Message on the Day of Prayer for Creation, 1 September 1994," repr., http://www.goarch.org/ourfaith/our faith8151.

of the gospel to a world in which many faithful servants have multiplied the resources that God entrusted to them.[23]

Given the problems we have just enumerated, we would like to propose that a sober Orthodox approach to the environment requires not only a faithful reading of the Tradition but also a critical engagement with everyone working on environmental issues—not a facile adoption of activist principle or policy. Having said that, we do not offer this work primarily as a right-of-center or conservative response to the existing body of Orthodox writing on the environment, for we all have much in common. We freely acknowledge our bias in favor of market-based approaches to environmental problems precisely because we care deeply that there be *results* from these policies that can genuinely improve the world, not merely provide us with good feelings because "we care." Thus, it is important to preserve endangered species, not merely make a statement that we wish to do so.[24]

The real environmental problems we face require study and meditation; they are far more likely to be solved by technological progress than by mandates from politicians responding to

---

[23] See Matthew 25:14–30. For a clear explanation of how property rights multiply resources and so resolve the "Lockean Proviso" to leave "as much and as good for others," see David Schmidtz, "The Institution of Property," *Social Philosophy & Policy* (Summer 1994): 42–62, reprinted in David Schmidtz and Elizabeth Willott, eds., *Environmental Ethics: What Really Matters, What Really Works* (Oxford: Oxford University Press, 2002), 361–72.

[24] For example, the U.S. Endangered Species Act is a terrible failure if it is measured by the number of species it saved from extinction. See Jonathan Adler, ed., *Rebuilding the Ark: New Perspectives on Endangered Species Act Reform* (Washington, DC: AEI Press, 2011); Andrew Morriss and Richard L. Stroup, "Quartering Species: The 'Living Constitution,' the Third Amendment, and the Endangered Species Act," *Environmental Law* 30, no. 4 (2000): 769–809.

special interests. Neither will progress in solving environmental problems come about in response to naïve invocations of Orthodox Tradition, by (perhaps willful) ignorance of contemporary advances in economics, biology, and technology or a failure to take into account the political reality of a world in which public as well as private institutions have flaws stemming from the fallen nature of man.[25] Rather, we hope to present a reading of the Orthodox Tradition and apply the insights we find there to contemporary environmental issues in ways we think are faithful to the Tradition and that can advance the discussion of contemporary environmental issues in Christian terms. To that end, we will consider how God is related to the Creation, the central place of mankind in the created order, and the role of mankind in the care and ultimate salvation of the world. Our application of these principles will be enhanced by the consideration of insights from economics, political science, and other disciplines that provide us with insights into how actions play out in the context of the natural world and human institutions.

---

[25] *Pace* the *Bases of the Social Concept* 13.5.1, which says, "The ecological problems are essentially anthropological as they are generated by man, not nature. Therefore, answers to many questions raised by the environmental crisis are to be found in the human heart, not in the spheres of economy, biology, technology or politics."

II How God Is Related to the Creation

Cosmic Theology

As the contemporary Orthodox theologian Fr. Andrew Louth points out, "it is often claimed that one of the characteristics of Greek—or Orthodox—theology is that it possesses a 'cosmic' dimension."[1] That is to say, in patristic and contemporary Orthodox thought there is a recognition that theology has a breadth of concern that transcends a narrow focus on mankind and his needs. While the creation of man and his fall and redemption in Christ are, and have always been, central concerns in Orthodoxy, the Orthodox Church has situated its consideration for these human issues within a larger horizon that embraces the whole of creation and sees the work of Christ in—literally—cosmic terms. The church's "goal is not only the salvation of people in this world, but also the salvation and restoration of the world itself."[2] This cosmic horizon finds its scriptural basis in Paul's Epistle to the Romans, where he writes,

> Creation waits with eager longing for the revealing of the
> sons of God; for the creation was subjected to futility,

---

[1] Andrew Louth, *Maximus the Confessor*, ed. Carol Harrison (New York: Rutledge, 1996), 63.

[2] *Bases of the Social Concept*, 1.2.2.

not of its own will but by the will of him who subjected it in hope; because the creation itself will be set free from its bondage to decay and obtain the glorious liberty of the children of God. We know that the whole creation has been groaning in travail together until now. (Rom. 8:19–22)

The contemporary iconographer Aidan Hart expresses well the basis of the ecclesial dimension of Orthodox thought on the environment, when he says,

if we are to be true to the Gospel, all our practical work needs to be in the context of what has been called the "cosmic liturgy." Our ecological work needs to be part of what Paul calls "a plan for the fulness of time, to unite all things in him, things in heaven and things on earth" (Eph. 1:10), "for in him all things were created, in heaven and on earth, visible and invisible … all things were created through him and for him." (Col. 1:16, 17)[3]

The development of this "cosmic dimension" in Orthodox theology is one of the chief contributions that Orthodoxy can make to fellow Christians in contemporary environmental discussions, and so it will have a prominent place in this monograph.

Creation—A Trinitarian Act

The Orthodox Church affirms that creation was a free act of God. However, the Orthodox go a step further and say that creation is not simply an act of God but a cooperative act of the Holy Trinity—Father, Son, and Holy Spirit. For "in the

---

[3] Aidan Hart, "The Pain of the Earth: A Cry for Change," (paper given at the European Council of Churches' Christian Environmental Network Conference, Minsk, Belarus, May 29, 2001), http://www. orthodoxytoday.org/articles4/HartEnvironment.php.

beginning," when "God created the heavens and the earth," "the Spirit [*pneuma*] of God was moving over the face of the waters"[4] and God the Father spoke through his Word, and the creation came to be.[5] Indeed, St. Irenaeus of Lyons (d. ca. 202) calls the Son and the Spirit the "two hands" of God with which he formed the world,[6] and St. John of Damascus (d. 749) says,

---

[4] Technical Greek terms that appear in the text, including direct quotes from other authors, will be transliterated into Latin characters for simplicity's sake.

[5] See Genesis 1:1–2. The notion that God created everything is ubiquitous in Scripture. That God created through his Word is often found, for example, in Psalm 33:6, "By the word of the Lord the heavens were made, and all their host by the breath of his mouth"; Psalms 104:24, "O LORD, how manifold are thy works! In wisdom [i.e., in the Word of God] hast thou made them all; (note also the reference to the Spirit in v. 30: "When thou sendest forth thy Spirit, they are created"); see John 1:3. That God created *ex nihilo* is stated only once in the Old Testament, in 2 Macc. 7:28, "look at the heaven and the earth and see everything that is in them, and recognize that God did not make them out of things that existed."

[6] *Against Heresies*, 4.20.1. For those unfamiliar with Patristic citation, a standard, widely available collection of early Christian texts is J.-P. Migne's *Patrologia latina* in 221 volumes and *Patrologia graeca* in 165 volumes published serially in Paris in the mid-nineteenth century. Citations to this collection are given as PL for the Latin series or PG for the Greek, followed by the volume number, column number (each page has two columns), section (each column is marked in four sections, A, B, C, and D), and sometimes a line number (each section having about 15 lines). Thus, this quotation from St. Irenaeus would be cited as PG 7.1032B6, meaning that the original text can be found in the *Patrologia graeca*, volume 7, column 1032, section B, line 6. We will include the citation from Migne where possible.

Since, then, God, who is good and more than good, did not find satisfaction in self-contemplation, but in His exceeding goodness wished certain things to come into existence which would enjoy His benefits and share in His goodness, He brought all things out of nothing into being and created them, both what is invisible and what is visible. Yea, even man, who is a compound of the visible and the invisible. And it is by thought that He creates, and thought is the basis of the work, the Word filling it and the Spirit perfecting it.[7]

Or, as St. Basil the Great puts it,

When you consider creation I advise you to think first of Him who is the first cause of everything that exists: namely, the Father, and then of the Son, who is the creator, and then the Holy Spirit, the perfector.... The Originator of all things is One: He creates through the Son and perfects through the Holy Spirit.... Perceive these three: the Lord who commands, the Word who creates, and the Spirit who strengthens."[8]

These statements of the Fathers are perhaps most simply put in the Symbol of Faith (the Nicene Creed), which acknowledges that the Father is the "maker of heaven and earth, and of all things visible and invisible," the Son is he "through whom all things were made," and the Holy Spirit is "the giver of life."

---

[7] St. John of Damascus, *On the Orthodox Faith*, 2.2 (PG 94.864C10-65A5), cited in Metropolitan Hilarion (Alfeyev), *The Mystery of Faith: An Introduction to the Teaching and Spirituality of the Orthodox Church* (Crestwood, NY: St. Vladimir's Seminary Press, 2011), 43–44.

[8] St. Basil the Great, *On the Holy Spirit*, 16.38 (Crestwood, NY: St. Vladimir's Seminary Press, 1980), 62–63 (PG 32.136A15-B3, B9-10, C11-13).

Creation was not a necessary or spontaneous effect of God's nature but a free act of divine will that brought into existence beings radically different from God. Created beings are radically different because they are created and contingent creatures made by an uncreated and absolute God. God freely chose to create out of love, for he "brought creatures into being not because He had need of anything," writes St. Maximus the Confessor, "but so that they might participate in Him in proportion to their capacity and that He Himself might rejoice in His works [cf. Ps. 104:31], through seeing them joyful and ever filled to overflowing with His inexhaustible gifts."[9]

According to the Psalmist, God created the cosmos by his Word: "he spoke, and it came to be; he commanded, and it stood forth" (Ps. 33:9), and as he says through the Prophet Isaiah, "so shall my word be that goes forth from my mouth; it shall not return to me empty, but it shall accomplish that which I purpose" (Isa. 55:11). The Word of God, then, is effective and realizes what it is spoken to do. This tells us that God had a particular motive from which he created the world, and a particular purpose for which he created it, and because of this motive and purpose, the world has meaning.[10] Because its motive is from

---

[9] St. Maximus the Confessor, *Centuries on Charity* 3.46. *The Philokalia*, vol. 2., trans. and ed. G. E. H. Palmer, Philip Sherrard, and Kallistos Ware (London: Faber & Faber, 1981), 90. See also Christos Yannaras, *Elements of Faith: An Introduction to Orthodox Theology*, trans. Keith Schram (Edinburgh: T&T Clark, 1991), 47, "God is the fullness of existence and of life, and he wishes that all that exists participate in this fullness, that every existing thing be an expression of divine life, a participation in the community of love which constitutes the mode of existence of God, the Being of God."

[10] Dumitru Stăniloae, *The Experience of God: Orthodox Dogmatic Theology*. trans. and ed. Ioan Ionita and Robert Barringer, vol. 2,

God and its purpose is in God, the meaning of the world is not found within itself but transcends the created order.[11] In fact, everything that God does has one single transcendent purpose: to unite everyone and everything to himself. This purpose can be known to us because the world, having been created through the Word (*Logos*), is rational (*logikos*).

To say more of this cosmic dimension, it stands against what some have called the great heresy of the modern age, namely, the notion that the world has an existence and a meaning in and of itself, or that "nature" can somehow be considered apart from God or apart from "grace." This notion, that we and the world are "down here" while God is someplace "up there," while common in Western popular conceptions, both Christian and secular, is alien to Orthodox thought.[12] It is true that God is transcendent to his creation, but the transcendence of God must not lead us to forget that he is immanent in the world as well.

A starting point for considering how each person must treat God's creation is to remember that there is no place where God is not. As we say in a prayer which begins almost all Orthodox services, "O Heavenly King, the Comforter, the Spirit of Truth, *Who are everywhere present and fill all things*, Treasury of blessings, and Giver of Life.…" Thus each person bears an individual responsibility for caring for all of creation, for God is present

---

The World: Creation and Deification (Brookline, MA: Holy Cross Orthodox Press, 2000), 17.

[11] See Christos Yannaras, *Elements of Faith*, 47.

[12] Father Stephen Freeman, an Orthodox parish priest, developed on his blog site the idea that Western Christians live in a "two-storey" universe, where God and heaven are far removed, while Orthodox Christians live in a "one-storey" universe, where God and heaven are here and now and interpenetrate the world. He recently published his ideas in *Everywhere Present: Christianity in a One-Storey Universe* (Chesterton, IN: Conciliar Press, 2011).

in all of it. Keeping this principle in mind when making our choices about the environment brings clarity—one should no more dump waste material that would damage creation in a lake or river than one would dump it in a church. At the same time, this principle focuses attention on us as individuals and our choices. It is as insufficient to delegate responsibility for the environment to the state as it is to leave it to the state to keep a church clean. Moreover, we must be wary of absolutist statements about our interaction with creation. Keeping a church clean does not imply that we cannot burn incense in it during services. Similarly, we have been given a creation capable of bearing some of our impacts. Thus the natural action of streams cleanses them to some degree of human-caused "pollution"—a term too often left ambiguous when there is currently no consensus of definition—and damming a stream may provide water or power at some cost to the "environment," too often understood in exclusion of the human beings who inhabit it.

This concept of God's presence everywhere has much deeper meaning as well. The immanence of God, his presence in the created order, is taught in Orthodox theology,[13] and that means creation, being filled with the presence of God, cannot be minimized when talking about how we come to know God or about how we are saved, for creation has a place in the economy of salvation, too. We will come to these issues in their own place. First, we need to flesh out how God is present here and now in creation. To do that, we must say something about St. Maximus

---

[13] It is also taught in classical Western theology. See, for example, Thomas Aquinas, *Summa theologica* I, Q. 8, art. 1, response: "God is in all things; not, indeed, as part of their essence, nor as an accident; but as an agent is present to that upon which it works." Thomas Aquinas, *Summa Theologica*, trans. Fathers of the English Dominican Province (Bellingham, WA: Logos Bible Software, 2009).

the Confessor and his theory about the Logos and the *logoi*, and about St. Gregory Palamas and his distinction between the essence and the energies of God.

St. Maximus—Logos and *Logoi*

St. Maximus the Confessor (d. 622) was a Byzantine monk and theologian who gained the epithet of "Confessor" for losing his life in defense of Orthodoxy during the christological controversies of the seventh century. He is important to our discussion—indeed central—because he refuted the false cosmology of Origen (d. 254), which was circulating in his day, a cosmology that taught the preexistence of souls and their subsequent embodiment in matter as a result of the fall. As part of his refutation, he wrote extensively on the theological and christological aspects of creation, the place of creation in the scheme of human salvation, and the centrality of man in the created order.[14]

Maximus states straightforwardly, "Always and in all the Word of God and God wills to effect the mystery of His embodiment."[15] The Word, the Logos, is embodied in the world and creates the world by means of certain *logoi* ("words," "reasons," or "principles") that come from him. These *logoi* are the "predeterminations" or "products of the divine will" by which he creates everything and imparts to everything its

---

[14] Hans Urs von Balthasar argues that Maximus "is the most world-affirming thinker of all the Greek Fathers." *Cosmic Liturgy: The Universe According to Maximus the Confessor* (San Francisco: Ignatius Press, 2003), 61. In citing Maximus, we are not breaking new ground; he is widely quoted by other Orthodox authors who write on environmental issues.

[15] *Ambiguum* 7 (PG 91.1084C15-D2).

unique characteristics.[16] Maximus does not understand the *logoi* to be a collection of ideal Platonic forms in the mind of God, nor should we understand the Logos himself to be a kind of divine reservoir chock full of little *logoi* waiting to burst forth into creation. On the contrary, the Logos remains one, simple and uncompounded, as befits God. The act of creation itself is the differentiation of the *logoi*, which become multiple in creation while remaining one and simple in the divine Logos. When God wills something or someone into existence, Peter for example, the *logos* of Peter is "spoken" by God and Peter comes to be. The *logos* of Peter has three aspects:

1. It is the cause of his existence, for prior to God saying, "*fiat* Peter," there was no Peter to speak of.

2. It is the principle of Peter's being, or the definition of what he is according to nature—not merely *a generic person*, but this particular man we call Peter.

3. It also includes the divine intention or purpose for which God created Peter, for, as we said, God's single purpose is to unite everything and everyone to himself, and Peter has a place in that divine purpose.

---

[16] *Ambiguum* 7 (PG 91.1085A), *On the Cosmic Mystery of Jesus Christ: Selected Writings from St. Maximus the Confessor*, trans. and intro. Paul M. Blowers and Robert Louis Wilken. (Crestwood, NY: St. Vladimir's Seminary Press, 2003), 61. St. Maximus is not the first of the Fathers to speak of the *logoi* of creation. See, for example, St. Gregory of Nyssa, *Apologia in Hexaemeron* 5 (PG 44.73A16-B1), "We should believe that in every existent thing there is a certain inner principle (or "word"), wise and full of artistry, even though it may surpass our vision." Cited in Anestis G. Keselopoulos, *Man and the Environment; A Study of St. Symeon the New Theologian*. trans. Elizabeth Theokritoff (Crestwood, NY: St. Vladimir's Seminary Press, 2001), n. 2, 104.

It is important not to think of the *logoi* as things that exist in themselves and that are different from the divine Logos and from the creatures they cause and define. They are not. They are simply *the immanence of the divine Wisdom, the Word of God, in created beings.* Because the Word/Logos of God is at the same time the cause and source of all of the *logoi* in creation when they come to be, sustains them in existence, and is their ultimate purpose, the Logos is *the* unifying, all-embracing cosmic Presence, "everywhere present and filling all things," but who is not embraced nor circumscribed by anything. To cite the Confessor,

> Through this Logos there came to be both being and continuing-to-be, for from him the things that were made came to be in a certain way and for a certain reason, and by continuing-to-be and by moving, they participate in God. For all things, in that they came to be from God, participate proportionally in God, whether by intellect [angels], by reason [humans], by sense perception [animals], by vital motion [plants], or by some habitual fitness [minerals].[17]

In this way, then, Maximus says the Word of God is embodied in creation. A clear theology of the presence of God in creation is important because it allows us to speak of God's immanence in the world in a way that does not lead us into pantheism, nor into the errors of the so-called "deep ecologists" who deify nature or worship "Gaia."[18] The Orthodox should thus be wary of what

---

[17] *Ambiguum* 7 (PG 91.1080B4-10), Paul Blowers and Robert Wilken, 55.

[18] Robert Nelson has written of environmentalism as a version of "Calvinism without God." See Robert H. Nelson, *The New Holy Wars: Economic Religion versus Environmental Religion in*

deep ecologist philosopher Arne Naess calls that approach's "comprehensive religious and philosophical worldview."[19]

Orthodox theology has always maintained that created beings differ in nature from God. Creation is not an emanation or "pouring out" of God so that creation itself is divine. It is not. St. Athanasius the Great (d. 373) puts it bluntly: Creation "is not the least like its Creator in substance, but is outside of him."[20]

However, "in creation" is not the only way the Word is embodied. The Confessor, in fact, speaks of three embodiments of the Logos: (1) in creation (through the *logoi*), (2) in the Scriptures, and (3) finally in the flesh in his incarnation as Jesus Christ.[21] As contemporary theologian Lars Thunberg points out,

> This three-fold incarnation seems to be closely linked with Maximus' idea of three general laws in the world: natural law, written law, and the law of grace. Thus, in Maximus' view, the Logos, on account of his general will to incarnate himself, holds together not only the *logoi* of creation but also the three aspects of creation, revelation (illumination), and salvation.
>
> Consequently, contemplation of the *logoi* in creation (*theōria physikē*) belongs to the work of the Spirit in man's sanctification and deification. This intellectual process

---

Contemporary America (University Park, PA: Pennsylvania State University Press, 2010).

[19] Bill Devall and George Sessions, *Deep Ecology: Living as if Nature Mattered* (Layton, UT: Gibbs M. Smith, 2001), 65.

[20] St. Athanasius the Great of Alexandria, *Against the Arians* 1.20 (PG 26.53A8-10), cited in Metr. Hilarion (Alfeyev), *The Mystery of Faith*, 43.

[21] See, for example, *Ambiguum* 33 (PG 91.1285C-1288A) and *Questions to Thalassius* 15 (PG 90.297B-300A).

is not separated from spiritual growth but is an integral part of it.[22]

We will take up the significance of natural contemplation later. For the moment, we can note that in Maximus' Logos/*logoi* theory we have an Orthodox analog of the Western notion of natural law, and to contemplate nature (that is, to perceive the *logoi* inherent in things) leads us to the Word of God himself, just like contemplation of Scripture does. This valorization of creation as a means of revelation *vis-à-vis* Scripture may be surprising, but it speaks of the high regard in which Orthodoxy holds natural theology, for nature is part of the means of our salvation.[23]

Thus, the Word of God is manifested through the creation, the Scriptures, and his incarnation in the flesh. Not only the Scriptures but each person and thing is a revelation of God, a *theophany*, a "showing forth" of God, and it is possible to see God in everyone and everything and to see everyone and everything in God. Here we may recall the well-known lines of the great fourth-century ascetic and founder of monasticism, St. Anthony the Great:

> A certain member of what was then considered the circle of the wise once approached the just Antony and asked him: "How do you ever manage to carry on, father,

---

[22] Lars Thunberg, *Microcosm and Mediator: The Theological Anthropology of Maximus the Confessor*, Acta Seminarii Neotestamentici Upsaliensis 25 (Copenhagen: C.W.K. Gleerup, Lund, & Einar Munksgaard, 1965), 82. The discussion of the three laws is found in *Questions to Thalassius* 64 (PG 90.724C).

[23] Thus Dumitru Stăniloae can begin his masterful work of dogmatic theology with the bald statement, "The Orthodox Church makes no separation between natural and supernatural revelation." *The Experience of God* (Boston: Holy Cross Press, 1994), 1.

deprived as you are of the consolation of books?" His reply: "My book, sir philosopher, is the nature of created things, and it is always at hand when I wish to read the words of God."[24]

Furthermore those of St. Augustine of Hippo:

Some people read books in order to find God. Yet there is a great book, the very appearance of created things. Look above you; look below you! Note it; read it! God, whom you wish to find, never wrote that book with ink. Instead, He set before your eyes the things that He had made. Can you ask for a louder voice than that? Why, heaven and earth cry out to you: "God made me!"[25]

The key to all of this is the Word himself. As Maximus says,

The mystery of the incarnation of the Logos is the key to all the arcane symbolism and typology in the Scriptures, and in addition gives us knowledge of created things, both visible and intelligible. He who apprehends the mystery of the cross and burial [of Christ] apprehends the inward essences of created things; while he who is initiated into

---

[24] Quoted in Evagrius of Pontus, *Praktikos* 92, *Evagrius Ponticus: Praktikos, Chapters on Prayer,* trans. John Eudes Bamberger, Cistercian Studies 4 (Kalamazoo: Cistercian Press, 2006), 39. The story also appears in Socrates, *Ecclesiastical History* 4.23 (PG 67.517; NPNF[2] 2:107), and it is cited in Kallistos Ware, *The Orthodox Way* (Crestwood, NY: St. Vladimir's Seminary Press, 1979), 43.

[25] Vernon J. Bourke, trans. and ed., *The Essential Augustine* (Indianapolis: Hackett, 1974), 123. The text is from *Sermon* 126.6 in the Angelo Mai collection of Augustine's sermons, *Miscellanea Agustiniana* 1:355-68, ed. G. Morin (Rome, 1930). It does not appear in Migne. There are several incorrect citations for the source of this quotation floating around the Internet.

the inexpressible power of the resurrection apprehends the purpose for which God first established everything.[26]

Indeed, in ways beyond all expectation, Jesus is the answer.

We point out all of this because it underscores part of the Orthodox approach to every issue, not only environmental ones: everything is approached holistically.[27] That means we cannot rightly understand the creation—including man and his place in it—if we do not rightly understand the Scriptures and if we do not live spiritual lives. Again, commenting on what it means "to grope after and discover God" (Acts 17:27), the Confessor says,

He who "gropes after God" properly has discretion (*diakrisis*). Therefore, he who comes upon the [Scriptures'] symbols intellectually (*gnōstikōs*), and who contemplates the phenomenal nature of created things scientifically (*epistēmonikōs*), discriminates within scripture, creation, and himself. He distinguishes, that is, between the letter (*gramma*) and the spirit (*pneuma*) in scripture, between the inner principle (*logos*) and the outward appearance (*epiphaneia*) in creation, and between the intellect (*nous*) and sense (*aisthēsis*) in himself, and in turn unites his own intellect indissolubly with the spirit of scripture and the inner principle of creation. Having done this, he "discovers God." For he recognizes, as is necessary and possible, that God is in the mind, and in the inner principle, and in the spirit; yet he is fully removed from everything misleading, everything that drags the mind down into countless opinions, in other words, the letter [of scripture], the appearance [of creation], and his own sense.... If someone mingles and confuses the letter of

---

[26] *Theological and Economic Centuries* 1.66, *The Philokalia*, vol. 2, 127.

[27] As we shall see below, the holistic Orthodox view is typically described as a *doxological* one, that is, one rooted in worship, in liturgy, and that incorporates both an ecclesial and an ascetical, communal and personal aspect.

> the [scripture], the outward appearance of visible things,
> and his own sense with one another, he "is blind and
> short-sighted" (2 Peter 1:9) and suffers from ignorance
> of the true Cause of created beings [God].[28]

What this means is that someone who does not rise to the fullness of scriptural understanding—to the spiritual meaning of the Scriptures—but relies on the letter alone, will suffer in his understanding of creation and in the progress of his spiritual life. Similarly, someone who does not transcend the outward appearance of created things will suffer in his understanding of Scripture and stumble in his spiritual progress, and someone who does not make progress in his spiritual life will suffer in his understanding of creation and of the Scriptures.[29]

The implications for environmental issues are clear: Those who would rightly understand creation—even through scientific investigation of it—must penetrate the outward appearances of creation and discern their *logoi*. They must also rightly understand the Scriptures, getting beyond the letter to their spiritual meaning; and they must live lives of spiritual integrity,

---

[28] *Question to Thalassius* 32 (PG 90.372.C4-D7), quoted in Paul M. Blowers, *Exegesis and Spiritual Pedagogy in Maximus the Confessor: An Investigation into the Quaestiones ad Thalassium*, Christianity and Judaism in Antiquity 7 (Notre Dame: University of Notre Dame Press, 1991), 100–101.

[29] See also St. Athanasius the Great, *On the Incarnation* 57.1–2; and the contemporary Elder Paisios (d. 1994) of Mount Athos: "Evil starts when the mind concentrates only on science and is totally separated from God. This is why it is difficult for people who think this way to find inner peace and balance. By contrast, when the mind revolves around God, and is illumined and sanctified, science is used both for our spiritual edification and for the benefit of the world." *Spiritual Counsels I: With Pain and Love for Contemporary Man* (Suroti, Thessaloniki, Greece: Holy Monastery "Evangelist John the Theologian," 2007), 228–29.

which in Orthodox terms, means diligently working through the classical stages of the active and contemplative life, that is, the stages of purification, illumination, and union with God.[30] These are all necessary and interrelated because all three are rooted in, and strive toward, the Word of God, who, being both their ground and their goal, unites them all in himself, the One who is, in fact, the truth. Failure to discern the *logoi* of creation results in a stunted view of the world, one that lays it open for abuse as something having no reference beyond itself. If creation has no transcendent meaning, then it is merely a thing, something ready-to-hand, able to be used thoughtlessly or exploited. Moreover, neglecting spiritual progress means living lives subject to bondage in sin, where appetite is not subject to reason and where neglect or abuse of God, neighbor, and creation become all too common. On the other hand, we must also avoid the parallel error of finding "meaning" solely within creation, as suggested by *Earth First!* Founder David Brower, who sees wilderness as the place where "there's still meaning."[31] Wilderness is not a place to develop "a pantheist-like vision of shared essence" but instead a place to grow closer

---

[30] As Scripture has it, we are called to be partakers of the divine nature (2 Peter 1:4), not mere imitators of Christ or simply followers of him. This union with God, which Scripture calls our glorification, has variously been called by the church fathers *deification*, *theosis*, and *transfiguration*. It is a very large issue and beyond the scope of what we can cover here.

[31] Susan Zakin, *Coyotes and Town Dogs: Earth First! and the Environmental Movement* (New York: Viking Press, 1993), 62. Brower sought to create "a way to make complete freedom work on a social scale, by setting up a community that would be small and tribal, with its own rituals and agreements, spoken and unspoken, shifting if necessary, but never coerced."

to God.[32] Experiencing God's creation must therefore not be a vehicle to develop "a new value system based on ecology and reverence for life," as the organizers of the first Earth Day hoped it would be,[33] but instead it must be a way to enrich our relationship with him.

St. Gregory Palamas—
Essence and Energies in God

A further Orthodox explanation of how God is present in the world is taken from the thought of St. Gregory Palamas, who was Archbishop of Thessalonica in the early fourteenth century and who wrote some spirited defenses of the monks on Mount Athos and their method of prayer. Gregory's explanation is commonly cited in Orthodox environmental writings as well.

Palamas elaborated a distinction between the *essence* of God and what he called his *energies* or *activities*. We know that God is transcendent and unknowable in his essence, and yet St. Peter tells us that we must become "partakers of the divine nature" (2 Peter 1:4). How can we reconcile these two seeming incompatible ideas? How can we know the unknowable, see the unseeable, and participate in the unparticipable?

St. Gregory says that we do these things when *we become by grace what God is by essence*. The grace of God that we receive is not separate from or different from God. Grace is simply God himself who makes himself available to our experience. As St. Gregory says, "Since we can participate in God and since the superessential essence of God is absolutely imparticipable, there [must be] something between imparticipable essence and

---

[32] Linda H. Graber, *Wilderness as Sacred Space*, Monograph Series 8 (Washington, DC: Association of America Geographers, 1976), 12.

[33] Susan Zakin, 37 (quoting Denis Hayes).

the participants, allowing them to participate in God."[34] This "something between" is not another God but what Gregory calls the creative and providential energies of God himself. Thus God creates everything by manifesting and sharing forth his energies—that is, his being, goodness, truth, beauty, life, and so on—and he is fully present in each of them. Everything in creation exists by sharing in and manifesting God's energies: created things are beautiful by sharing in and manifesting God's beauty; true by sharing in and manifesting God's truth; good by sharing in and manifesting God's goodness; and so forth. This means, again, that every created thing can be a theophany—a revelation of God.

What does this say about nature? About any creature? It says that nothing is simply an object to be used, an inert, meaningless thing. Everything, every creature—from spotted owls to veins of coal in a mountain—shares in the energies of God. It says that somehow God is present and can be discerned there, if we can see, not only with our eyes but also with our hearts. How we can see the world in this way is through natural contemplation (*thēoria physikē*), which we will consider below. We must also remember that Christianity is not Jainism—we are not called to gently sweep insects from our paths for fear of inadvertently stepping on one. Rather we are called to *stewardship*, an active role in which we must do more than *preserve* what God has given to us but responsibly and prayerfully *use* it in pursuit of our responsibilities to God and our brothers and sisters. Sometimes a good steward husbands a resource. Sometimes, however, a good steward makes use of a resource in pursuit of the steward's call-

---

[34] *Triads in Defense of the Holy Hesychasts* 3.2.24 in *Grégoire Palamas: Défense des saints hésychastes*, 2nd ed., ed. and trans. Jean Meyendorff; Études et Documents 30 and 31, vol. 31 (Leuven: Spicilegium Sacrum Lovaniense, 1973), 687. The English translation here is our own.

ing. Orthodox environmentalism cannot thus be a static vision of nature as something to be preserved unaltered. A steward's task is much harder than either digging up every last lump of coal or refraining from touching any of it. In entrusting us with responsibility for the natural world, God gave us opportunities to exercise judgment, not a simplistic recipe. While life would surely be simpler if he asked less of us, it would leave us as less than he intended us to be.

III Humanity's Place in Creation —Microcosm

St. Maximus teaches, "The whole world, made up of visible and invisible things, is a man, and conversely … man, made up of body and soul, is a world."[1] That is to say, there is a reciprocal relationship between man and the world. Man is a microcosm (*microcosmos*), a "little world" because he is both visible and invisible, made up of body and soul, a unity in diversity just like the world is. The Eastern Fathers of the fourth century took up this idea from the ancient Greek philosophers and reinterpreted it in a Christian context.[2] St. Gregory of Nyssa is particularly clear when he describes the microcosmic composition of man:

> While two natures—the Divine and incorporeal nature, and the irrational life of brutes—are separated from each other as extremes, human nature is the mean between them; for in the compound nature of man we may behold a part of each of the natures I have mentioned—of the Divine, the rational and intelligent element [of the soul] … of the irrational, our bodily form and structure.[3]

---

[1] *Mystagogy* 7 (PG 91.684D12-85A1), George C. Berthold, trans., *Maximus Confessor: Selected Writings* (New York: Paulist Press, 1985), 196.

[2] A *locus classicus* is Plato's *Timaeus* 81A, D.

[3] St. Gregory of Nyssa, *On the Making of Man*, 16.9 in *NPNF*² 5:404 (PG 44.181B13-C7). See also St. John of Damascus, *On the Orthodox Faith*, 2.12.1 (PG 94.920A).

Because man is made of a rational soul, he is like the incorporeal, spiritual nature of the angels, who also share a likeness to the rational God. At the same time, having a body, he is like everything in the physical order as well. This gives man a unique place in the creation for he is the only creature that shares both realms and is therefore the only creature fit to be called a microcosm of the whole creation[4] standing in the middle between the incorporeal and the corporeal.

Even the order of creation as presented in the first chapter of Genesis points to the centrality of mankind in the cosmos. After describing the creation of the universe on the first and second days of creation, the focus from day three onward is geocentric. As Metropolitan Hilarion (Alfeyev) of Volokolamsk notes, "this has profound symbolic meaning." He goes on to quote the Russian theologian Vladimir Lossky (d. 1958), who says,

> This is not a residue of primitive cosmology ... which would keep faith with our post-Copernican universe. For this is not a physical geocentrism, but a spiritual one: the earth is spiritually central because it is the body of man, and because man ... is the central being of creation, the being who reunites in himself the sensible and the intelligible and thus participates, richer than the angels, in all the orders of "earth" and "heaven." At the center of the universe beats the heart of man.[5]

---

[4] At the same time, because of his freewill, he transcends both parts of his nature. Not surprisingly, we find the same idea of man as a microcosm in St. Maximus. Thunberg notes that the Confessor's understanding of man as a microcosm is "a dominant element in Maximus' general anthropology" (*Microcosm and Mediator*, 140). See 140–50 for a full treatment; also von Balthasar, *Cosmic Liturgy*, 171–77.

[5] Metr. Hilarion (Alfeyev), *The Mystery of Faith*, 53–54, quoting Vladimir Lossky, *Orthodox Theology: An Introduction* (Crestwood,

The classic statement of man's place in creation is found in St. Gregory the Theologian (d. 389) and repeated verbatim by St. John of Damascus several centuries later. Man, made from both corporeal and incorporeal natures, is

> a great cosmos in miniature; another angel, a "hybrid" worshiper, a full initiate (or: overseer) of the visible creation and initiated also into the intelligible creation; a king of things on earth, but subject to the King above.... A creature trained here and en route to somewhere else, and—the ultimate mystery—deified by its tendency toward God.[6]

Both incorporeal and corporeal natures are united in man for "everything created by God is good, and nothing is to be rejected if it is received with thanksgiving"; as the apostle says in 1 Timothy 4:4, "for then it is consecrated by the word of God," which is to say that *man is a microcosm, not simply to embody in himself the whole creation but so that the whole creation might be saved along with him*, that is, "in order that the earthly might be raised up to the Divine that the one grace might pervade the whole creation."[7] Man's role, then, as *microcosm* is in service to his role as *mediator* of the salvation of the whole creation. That is, the idea of man as microcosm is linked to a task of mediation, of unifying through himself the disparate elements of creation.

NY: St. Vladimir's Seminary Press, 2001), 64.

6   Cited in Elizabeth Theokritoff, *Living in God's Creation: Orthodox Perspectives on Ecology* (Crestwood, NY: St. Vladimir's Seminary Press, 2009), 67–68. The texts of St. Gregory the Theologian she cites are *Homily 38, On Theophany*, 11 and *Homily 45, On Pascha*, 7. The corresponding passage in St. John of Damascus is in *On the Orthodox Faith*, 2.12.4.

7   See Elizabeth Theokritoff, *Living in God's Creation*, 67, citing St. Gregory of Nyssa, *Great Catechism* 6 (PG 45.25D5-7, 28A3-4).

Man is not simply to *be* a microcosm, as an image or icon of the world; rather, he is to *function* as one, as well: to gather up into himself all the varied elements of the created order, mortal and immortal, rational and irrational beings, and so forth, as well as to offer them up to God.[8]

This idea is most extensively spelled out by St. Maximus, and thus we will briefly summarize his theory. Maximus says that in the incarnation of Christ, God accomplished the cosmic task of recapitulating all of creation and drawing it back to himself. This task had been given to Adam in the beginning, but because of the fall and its resulting effects in corruption and death, division and separation had been introduced into the world instead. Thus handicapped, Adam was unable to realize his role in the divine plan. Christ, however, by assuming human nature and restoring it to its original function, was himself able to accomplish this cosmic task, and each person regenerated in the Church and baptized into Christ is empowered to do the same. This task involves overcoming all the division and separation in the created order and unifying it and offering it back to God.

In *Ambiguum* 41, Maximus develops a theory of how everything is divided.[9] He distinguishes being into five pairs. From higher to lower, being is distinguished between the Uncreated

---

[8] Lars Thunberg, *Man and the Cosmos: The Vision of St. Maximus the Confessor* (Crestwood, NY: St. Vladimir's Seminary Press, 1985), 73.

[9] Found also in *Questions to Thalassius* 48 and 63, we focus on the text of *Ambiguum* 41 here. The most exhaustive treatment of this idea in Maximus is found in Thunberg, *Microcosm and Mediator*, 396–454. See also, idem., *Man and the Cosmos*, 80–91; Andrew Louth, *Maximus the Confessor*, 72–74; and Torstein Theodor Tollefsen, *The Christocentric Cosmology of St. Maximus the Confessor*, Oxford Early Christian Studies (Oxford, New York: Oxford University Press, 2008), 82–83.

(God) and all created natures; created nature is distinguished into intelligible and sensible; sensible nature into heaven and earth, earth into paradise and the inhabited world (Gk. *oikoumenē*); and the inhabited world into male and female. Man is able to perform the task of reconciling these pairs because he is a *microcosm* and serves as a "kind of natural bond" (*syndesmos tis physikos*)[10] between all of the distinguished pairs. That is to say, each person is also called to be a *mediator* among them all: "they belong in paradise but inhabit the inhabited world; they are earthly and yet destined for heaven; they have both mind and senses; and though created, they are destined to share in the uncreated nature by deification."[11]

The task of reconciling the distinctions begins with the last pair and proceeds in reverse order to the first pair. The division between the sexes is transcended through living virtuously, for in Christ there is neither male nor female, as St. Paul says in Galatians 3:28. The division between paradise and the inhabited earth—which is most important and to which we shall return—is transcended by a "way of life proper and fitting to the Saints." Then, by imitating the life of the angels, the division between heaven and earth is overcome. Next, by perceiving the *logoi* of things through natural contemplation, the distinction between the intelligible and sensible is resolved. Finally, by uniting created nature with the uncreated God through love, the interpenetration (*perichōrēsis*) of God and creation is revealed.[12] All of these distinctions are resolved by a person making progress through the classical stages of the spiritual life. Note that, according to Maximus, the resolution of the first three distinctions (between male and female, paradise

---

[10] *Ambiguum* 41, PG 91.1305B14.

[11] Andrew Louth, *Maximus the Confessor* (London & New York: Routledge, 1996), 73.

[12] Louth, *Maximus Confessor*, 73.

and the inhabited earth, heaven and earth) are all proper to the *practical* life, the *active* life; only the resolution of the latter two, that is, intelligible and sensible, and the uncreated and created, belong to the *contemplative* life. This means that environmental concerns—which we submit are bound up with the reconciliation of paradise and the inhabited earth—are a *practical* matter, not a theoretical or contemplative one, accomplished through "a way of life proper and fitting to the Saints." We will return to the five distinctions later.

The Confessor also reiterates the idea that "the soul is a middle being between God and matter and has powers that can unite it with both, that is, it has a mind that links it with God and senses that link it with matter,"[13] but he goes further in tying the role of man as microcosm with the notion that the world is a *macranthropos*, that is, a "large man," or perhaps better put, "man writ large." As we quoted him above, "the whole world, made up of visible and invisible things, is a man, and conversely … man, made up of body and soul, is a world."[14] That is to say, in the Confessor's thought,

soul : body :: incorporeal world : corporeal world

As there is only one human nature comprised of body and soul, so also there is only one creation comprised of its different elements. Man is a *microcosm* of creation and creation is a *macranthropos* of man.[15]

We can say this much here: that the composite human person and the composite creation are images of each other is not a difficult concept. Having made clear that man is a microcosm,

---

[13] *Ambiguum* 10 (PG 91.1193D), Louth, *Maximus the Confessor*, 147.

[14] *Mystagogy*, 7 (PG 91.684D-85A), Berthold, *Maximus Confessor*, 196.

[15] Lars Thunberg, *Man and the Cosmos*, 74.

we now further explore his role as mediator in the salvation of the world.

We have cited Lossky who says that "the earth is spiritually central because it is the body of man, and because man … is the central being of creation"; and we have seen Maximus say that "the whole world … is man, and conversely … man … is a world." The great Romanian theologian Fr. Dumitru Stăniloae (d. 1993) pushes these ideas a step further to underscore the centrality of man in creation. He says that *man is not a part of creation at all, but rather that creation is a part of man*: "It is not that man is a part of the cosmos, but that all the parts of the cosmos are parts of man. Man is not a microcosm sided by a macrocosm, nor is he framed within a macrocosm, but he is the actual cosmos, as he gives a complete unity and a complete meaning to all the parts of creation."[16] This is because the creation is not of itself personal; that is to say, it has its own nature, to be sure, but it has no personhood, no *hypostasis* of its own. Adam was intended to serve as the microcosm of the world, but, as we said, through the fall, he lost the ability to fulfill this cosmic task. Christ, through his passion, death, and resurrection fulfilled it, and man, united to Christ in baptism, is able to fulfill it now. Thus, Christian teaching stands in opposition (1) to those "deep ecologists" who claim that nature has its own

---

[16] Dumitru Stăniloae, note 328 to St. Maximus the Confessor, *Ambigua* 41 (PG 91.1308B-C). *Părinți și Scritori Bisericești* 80 (București, EIBMBOR, 1983), 262, cited in Dragos Bahrim, "The Anthropic Cosmology of St. Maximus the Confessor," *Journal for Interdisciplinary Research on Religion and Science*, 2008, no. 3, 28. The same idea is found in Stăniloae's contemporary, Paul Evdokimov, "Man is placed at the summit of this living whole as a synthesis of the spiritual and the material. In its organic continuity the cosmos appears as the surface of the extended human body, and the saints take their place as the hypostases of cosmic nature," "Nature," *Scottish Journal of Theology* 18 (1965): 3.

hypostasis/personhood (i.e., "Gaia"); (2) to pantheists who claim that nature is God; and (3) to animists who claim that there are all kinds of deities animating creation.[17]

In light of this teaching that creation is a part of man, an Orthodox view of the world cannot be simply "creation-centered," taking no account of God or of man nor can it be simply "anthropocentric," taking less account of God or creation, but somehow it must take into account God, mankind, and the rest of creation all at once and hold all these elements together at the same time. Moreover, it cannot be reduced to the idea of pioneering American environmentalist Aldo Leopold's "land

---

[17] This point is particularly important in interacting with contemporary environmentalists. Professor Lynn White Jr.'s influential 1967 article, "The Historical Roots of Our Ecological Crisis," explicitly blamed environmental problems on Christianity, which he termed "the most anthropocentric religion the world has seen." Lynn White Jr., "The Historical Roots of Our Ecological Crisis," *Science* 155 (1967): 1203. White argued that pre-Christian religions fostered reverence for nature. He went on to note that pre-Christian beliefs often included animistic beliefs in "guardian spirits" of hills, streams, and trees. "Before one cut a tree, mined a mountain, or dammed a brook, it was important to placate the spirit in charge of that particular situation, and to keep it placated." He argued that Christianity's destruction of animism's belief in local guardian spirits "made it possible to exploit nature in a mood of indifference to the feelings of natural objects." As a result, he contended "we shall continue to have a worsening ecologic crisis until we reject the Christian axiom that nature has no reason for existence save to serve man." His argument that returning to pre-Christian religious beliefs about nature would be environmentally beneficial is not uncommon. White's article is not merely a rant about theology. It was published in *Science*, one of the preeminent scientific journals and remains a foundational document for much of modern environmental thought.

ethic" in which "the role of *Homo sapiens* [shifts] from conqueror of the land-community to plain member and citizen of it."[18] Man is more than simply a citizen of creation—he is a steward, called to actively participate in God's creation in fulfillment of God's plan.

Excursus: Is Creation an Icon?

Given this understanding of man's place in the creation as a microcosm and mediator, we can say whether or not nature is an icon of God. The question is worth considering because the incarnation of Christ shows us that matter can be sanctified and that flesh can be transfigured. It is also worth considering because many people associate the Orthodox Church with icons and so Orthodox writers often use them as illustrations of Orthodox concepts, including environmental ones.

An icon (Gk. *eikon* = "image"), in Orthodox understanding, is not a naturalistic representation of some object. Icons are always images of *persons*, either of Christ—who is himself the image of God[19]—or of his saints—who are images of Christ (that is, images of the Image). Moreover, icons are not photographic representations. Rather, an icon depicts a person who has been transfigured by divine grace. That is why all of the figures shown in an icon are stylized: They are seen not as they are illumined *from without* by the natural light of the sun but rather as they are illumined *from within* by the uncreated light of God's grace. Indeed, Orthodox tradition recognizes the great iconographers as those who have become holy, who have achieved (at the least) natural contemplation, whose spiritual eyes are cleansed

---

[18] Aldo Leopold, *A Sand County Almanac* (Oxford: Oxford University Press, 1968), 215.

[19] See 2 Corinthians 4:4; Colossians 1:15; and Hebrews 1:3.

by grace so that they can perceive the transfigured world and depict it faithfully.[20]

Due to this interior illumination that is depicted in an icon, nature by itself and seen with an unillumined eye cannot be an icon of God. That is not to say that aspects of nature are never represented in icons. On the contrary, mountains, trees, bushes, animals, rivers, and many other aspects of the animal and mineral world are often depicted in icons; however, they are always background/secondary to the divine or human person who is the subject of the icon. Nature also needs grace because it shares in the fallen condition of mankind.

Because nature is a part of us, it is sanctified and becomes part of the image of God when we are sanctified and become part of the image (Christ) through incorporation into his body through baptism. Just as the central figure of an icon is stylized, the natural elements surrounding him and/or her are not shown naturally either but are themselves presented in a stylized way—their *logoi* are revealed—for they, too, are transfigured by the uncreated light of God's grace. "Through himself, man leads the whole creation to God."[21] That is why, for example, in some icons, mountains in the background "bow" toward the central figure of Christ; and why plants are sometimes

[20] Aidan Hart, *Beauty and the Gospel*,

> In reality the Church, through her iconographers, depicts the world as she really experiences it. This is why iconographers must be members of the Orthodox Church, chaste, and people of prayer; if icons are to be a genuine witness they must be painted by people who have seen what they are painting, and this is only possible through the Body of Christ.

Available at http://aidanharticons.com/wp-content/uploads/2012/08/Beauty-and-the-gospel.pdf.

[21] St. Gregory Palamas quoted in Paul Evdokimov in *The Art of the Icon* (Trabuco Canyon, CA: Oakwood Publications, 1990), 304.

depicted with golden leaves, transfigured and shot through, as it were, by the uncreated light of God's grace.[22] In short, when the creation is brought to God and transfigured, it attains its fulfillment, its *logoi* are revealed, and its harmony and balance are manifest and restored. Thus, nature can be an icon when its *logoi* are perceived and when it is seen with the eye of faith. Moreover, because an icon displays creation's *logoi*, revealing its God-intended purpose and fulfillment, its harmony and balance, it is not simply an illustration of what creation can be in the fullness of time. Rather, *an icon is the embodiment and manifestation of that reality here and now, and by making it real and present here and now, an icon itself becomes a means for the transfiguration of creation.* As an icon, nature is valued because it points us toward God and not for its own sake as many contemporary environmentalists believe.

Because of man's role as microcosm and mediator, all of creation finds its fulfillment when it is taken up in worship or referred to Christ in some way. As the Fathers and the hymnology of the Church point out, Christ himself healed human nature by his incarnation. He healed the waters of the earth by his baptism. He healed the air by his ascension through it. He

---

[22] Aidan Hart, "Transfiguring Matter: The Icon as Paradigm of Christian Ecology,"

> We notice that trees, mountains, birds are not depicted as a naturalist would: trees, especially in mosaics such as those in Ravenna, are shown flecked with gold, shot through with light as in their true Paradisical state; mountains bow towards the saints; birds often have colour combinations not seen in this world. The whole arrangement of each person and thing in an icon reveals the poetical harmony of a redeemed creation, each thing operating according to its inner logos or essence, inclining towards its Maker.

Available at http://aidanharticons.com/wp-content/uploads/2012/08/ICONECOL.pdf.

healed the relationship with animals during his forty days in the wilderness, when he was with the beasts, and when he sat on the donkey at his entrance into Jerusalem.[23]

This healing of nature, or its transfiguration, is not something that only Christ accomplishes. It is also something that the saints in every generation have been able to accomplish, as well. We recall from Scripture, for example, Joshua, son of Nun, praying for the sun to stand still, the prophet Elijah being fed by the raven, and the effect of Elisha's prayers on drought and rain.[24] The extraordinary relationships many saints have with animals is a hagiographical commonplace: Roman Catholics are familiar with stories of St. Francis of Assisi (d. 1226) taming the wolf of Gubbio and his sermon to the birds, St. Anthony of Padua's (d. 1231) sermon to the fish, St. Jerome (d. 420) and his lion, and St. Martin de Porres (d. 1639) and his rats. Orthodox Christians are familiar with the stories of St. Mammas (d. ca. 275) riding the lion, St. Pachomius (d. 346) crossing the Nile on the back of a crocodile, St. Sergius of Radonezh (d. 1392) and St. Seraphim of Sarov (d. 1833) and their bears, St. Innocent of Alaska (d. 1879) with his eagle, and many stories of contemporary monks and nuns living in peace with all kinds of wild things.[25] All of these stories point to a healed and transfigured

---

[23] See Mark 1:13 and Luke 19:29–36, note especially that the colt was one on which "no one has ever yet sat," that is, it was untamed.

[24] See Joshua 10:12–14; 1(3) Kings 17:1 and 18:41–45; and 1(3) Kings 17:4–6.

[25] For more examples, and a fuller discussion, see Elizabeth Theokritoff, "Saints and Their Environment," in *Living in God's Creation*, chap. 3, 117. Examples of twentieth-century Athonite monks living in such harmony can be found in Archimandrite Cherubim (Karambelas), *Contemporary Ascetics of Mount Athos*, 2 vols. (Platina, CA: St. Herman of Alaska Brotherhood Press, 1992).

creation restored to harmony with humanity directly as a result of the sanctification of human persons.

In addition to the transfiguration of nature by individual saints, the Church sanctifies matter corporately through its mysteries (sacraments) and prayers: bread and wine in the Eucharist, oil in Chrismation and Holy Unction, water in the Great Blessing of Water on Theophany; wooden boards and crushed pigments of minerals used to paint icons; resins for incense and beeswax for candles; and prayers for blessing homes, fields, seed, herds, flocks, and first fruits.[26] Thus, matter, indeed all of nature, is transfigured by human agency by being brought into the Church either through offering it in its liturgical life or through the contemplation of its *logoi*.

---

[26] Vigen Guroian speaks well of "the ecological ethic that emerges from a study of the rites of blessing" in the Orthodox Church. "Ecological Ethics: An Ecclesial Event," *Ethics After Christendom* (Grand Rapids: Eerdmans, 1994), 155–74.

IV Living in the Creation: An Orthodox Ethos

The brethren came to Abba Anthony and said to him, "Speak a word; how are we to be saved?" The old man said to them, "You have heard the Scriptures. That should teach you how." But they said, "We want to hear from you too, Father." Then the old man said to them, "The Gospel says, 'If anyone strikes you on one cheek, turn to him the other also.'" They said, "We cannot do that." The old man said, "If you cannot offer the other cheek, at least allow one cheek to be struck." "We cannot do that either," they said. So he said, "If you are not able to do that, do not return evil for evil," and they said, "We cannot do that either." Then the old man said to his disciple, "Prepare a little brew of corn for these invalids. If you cannot do this, or that, what can I do for you? What you need is prayers."[1]

Given the background we have laid out and the understanding of creation—God's relationship to it and man's place in it—we can now ask the question: How should we live in a way that is conscious of our place in creation? Can this Orthodox

---

[1] Abba Anthony, "Saying 19," in *The Desert Christian: The Sayings of the Desert Fathers, The Alphabetical Collection*, trans. Benedicta Ward (New York: Macmillan, 1975), 5.

perspective speak to environmental issues? We believe that it can and in a number of ways. Taking our cue from this saying of Abba Anthony, we suggest there is somewhat of a hierarchy of considerations in how we might approach environmental issues in this section. To begin with, we might simply wait for the second coming of Christ when creation will be healed and everything will be restored in the new heavens and earth, and Christ will be "all in all."[2] Perhaps we cannot and should not do that for many reasons, however.

So, in the next place, we suggest that everybody (including you, gentle reader) attain holiness so that we are not overcome by our passions and are not led to use the world—or each other—in sinful, selfish ways; nor, because of our distance from God and the darkness of our minds, will we stumble around without his illumination, which guides us in ways that are consistent with a proper use of the world according to its *logoi*. Orthodox Tradition bears clear witness to the possibility and effectiveness of this approach in the lives of the Saints. However if we want to address environmental issues in our day, perhaps that is too much to ask, at least in the short term.

Next, we suggest practicing natural contemplation so that, by discerning the *logoi* of things, our minds can ascend to the divine *Logos* himself, and, being illumined by grace, we can see how to use the things of the world properly—according to their God-intended *logoi*—and not abusively, that is, in ways that run contrary to God's will for them. Maybe we cannot do that either (though we will argue it is possible and reasonable, and to some degree necessary). Because we, too, are invalids and can only prepare "a little brew of corn" ourselves, we will begin with the most simple and practical matters and leave higher considerations for later.

---

[2] See Isaiah 65:17; Apocalypse 21:1–9; 1 Corinthians 15:28; and Ephesians 1:23.

We suggest that there are three possible ways of living in the creation in an environmentally responsible way: as a slave, as a servant, and as a son. With regard to living in the creation as a son, there are three aspects to be considered, which correspond to three traditional roles assigned to Christ, those of king, prophet, and priest. In developing this outline, we will be able to move from the most "practical" considerations, through those that are higher, to consider the highest role for mankind with regard to the creation, that of offering back to God, "Your own of Your own, in behalf of all and for all," as the Divine Liturgy says. To consider these ways of living responsibly in the creation, we must address two presuppositions beforehand: the ecclesial dimension of Orthodoxy's worldview, and the ascetical dimension of it.

Two Preliminary Considerations

The Ecclesial Dimension

The Fourth Ecumenical Council at Chalcedon (AD 451) defined the "hypostatic union," the definition of how Christ can be one person while being fully God and fully man at the same time. The core of the Chalcedonian definition says:

> one and the same Son, our Lord Jesus Christ: the same perfect in divinity and perfect in humanity, the same truly God and truly man, of a rational soul and a body; consubstantial with the Father as regards his divinity, and the same consubstantial with us as regards his humanity; … one and the same Christ, Son, Lord, only-begotten, acknowledged in two natures which undergo *no confusion, no change, no division, no separation*; at no point was the difference between the natures taken away through the union, but rather the property of both natures is

> preserved and comes together into a single person and a
> single subsistent being....[3]

We recall the definition of *Chalcedon* here because it is important to remember who Christ is when we consider what his body, the Church, is. The Church, like its head, is a *theandric* reality, that is, one that is both fully divine (*theo-*) and fully human (*-andros*) at the same time and that maintains both divine and human aspects without confusion, change, division, or separation between them. As the *Bases of the Social Concept* puts it,

> The Church is a divine-human organism. Being the body
> of Christ, she unites in herself the two natures, divine
> and human, with their inherent actions and wills. The
> Church relates to the world through her human, created,
> nature. However, she interacts with it not as a purely
> earthly organism but in all her mysterious fullness. It
> is the divine-human nature of the Church that makes
> possible the grace-giving transformation and purifica-
> tion of the world accomplished in history in the creative
> co-work, "synergy," of the members and the Head of the
> Church body.[4]

After the Council of Chalcedon, the terms *confusion*, *change*, *division*, and *separation* carry negative connotations in subsequent Orthodox thought.

> It is in these terms that Maximus describes the effects of
> the Fall on human beings and the cosmos, effects that do
> not alter the fundamental meaning (*logos*) of natures, but
> are to be found in the way fallen natures act and interact,
> so that confusion, division, and fragmentation obscure

---

[3] N. Tanner, ed., *Decrees of the Ecumenical Councils*, 2 vols. (London: Sheed & Ward; Washington DC: Georgetown University Press, 1990), 1:86–87. Emphasis added.

[4] *Bases of the Social Concept*, 1.2.1.

> the fundamental reality, disclosed by the *logos* of each nature, of what God has created.[5]

Thus, it is in the Church where confusion, change, division, and separation are overcome and reconciled, where humans and the whole created order find their fundamental meaning—their *logoi*—affirmed. The Church can accomplish this affirmation because it works the same effects as God does, "in the same way as the image reflects its archetype."[6] That is, "it realizes the same union of the faithful with God. As different as they are by language, place, and custom, they are made one by it through faith."[7] Moreover, as we saw earlier, just as "the whole world, made up of visible and invisible things, is a man, and conversely … man, made up of body and soul, is a world,"[8] so, too, does Maximus speak of the "Church as a figure and image of the entire world composed of visible and invisible essences because like it, it contains both unity and diversity."[9] Therefore we have a series of correspondences:

Soul : body (in the human person) ::

The incorporeal world : the corporeal world (in the created order) ::

Heaven : earth (in the created order) ::

Unity of faith : diversity of persons (in the Church).

---

[5] Andrew Louth, *Maximus the Confessor* (London & New York: Routledge, 1996), 50. That is to say, the fall affects not the logos of nature (*logos physeos*) of a thing, but its way or manner of being (*tropos hyparxeos*). More on this below.

[6] Maximus the Confessor, *Mystagogy* 1, in Berthold, *Maximus Confessor*, 187.

[7] *Mystagogy* 1, Berthold, *Maximus Confessor*, 188.

[8] *Mystagogy* 7, Berthold, *Maximus Confessor*, 196.

[9] *Mystagogy* 2, Berthold, *Maximus Confessor*, 188.

Each of these corresponds to each of the others, and all of them function according to the "Chalcedonian logic"—each pair is held together as one whole reality made up of different parts, which remain united in the whole without confusion, change, division, or separation.

This is important because it affirms *the persistent reality of every creature when it is incorporated into the Church and united to God*: nothing is lost or ceases to be. No part of the creation is cast aside or deemed unimportant.[10] Everything begins to shed the corruption and death that has marred it since the fall of man. In this way, the Church functions as a microcosm and a mediator gathering all of the cosmos into one orderly harmony and communion and referring it all to God. Paul tells us that "if any one is in Christ, he is a new creation" (2 Cor. 5:17). Because all the parts of the cosmos are parts of man, as we have seen, then as people are incorporated into Christ by entry into his Church, so also is the whole created order brought into the Church, and it, too, becomes a part of the new creation. This "churching" of creation takes place as each person freely cooperates with the unifying work of God's energies (i.e., grace):

> Once man helps himself through the renewing power of repentance, it is easy to remake the rest of creation in the proper way and bring it into the Church. The renewal of persons which precedes the renewal of the world is again accomplished in the Church. Through the Mysteries [Sacraments] and services of the Church, and also by studying the lives of the Saints that offer examples of renewal appropriate to each person, the believer is helped in the spiritual struggle for his own renewal and the churching of his environment.[11]

---

[10] We recall in passing Christ's command after the feeding of the five thousand, "Gather up the fragments left over, that nothing may be lost" (John 6:12).

[11] Keselopoulos, *Man and the Environment*, 154–55.

Or again, as the *Bases of the Social Concept* eloquently puts it, "… we tend to change the world around us in accordance with our own inner world; therefore, the transformation of nature should begin with the transformation of the soul. According to St. Maximus the Confessor, man can turn the earth into paradise only if he carries paradise within himself."[12] This ecclesial dimension is inherent in Orthodoxy's view of the world and its salvation, and we must presuppose it when we can consider the more individual dimension of personal asceticism.

The Ascetical Dimension

The second presupposition we need to address is the Orthodox view of asceticism. It is important to clarify the Church's teaching on asceticism because many voices in the environmental movement encourage a kind of ascetical lifestyle in the name of "ethical consumption." Orthodox writers on the environment are not immune to the temptation of putting the ascetical tradition of the Church in the service of another agenda. For example, the conclusion of the Inter-Orthodox Conference on Environmental Protection, held in Crete in 1991, states "Humanity needs a simpler way of life, a renewed asceticism, for the sake of creation."[13] Many Orthodox writers call on asceticism—fasting in particular—to reduce consumption.[14] Deacon Dr. John Chryssavgis, the theological advisor to the

---

[12] *Bases of the Social Concept*, 13.5.3.

[13] Article III, http://www.goarch.org/ourfaith/ourfaith8060.

[14] See, for example, Patriarch Bartholomew I of Constantinople, "Speech at the Environmental Symposium," Saint Barbara Greek Orthodox Church, Santa Barbara, CA (November 8, 1997); Metropolitan John (Zizioulas), "Ecological Asceticism: A Cultural Revolution," *Our Planet* 6, no. 7 (1996): 7, reprinted in *Sourozh* 67 (1997): 22–25; Elias Economou, "An Orthodox View of the Ecological Crisis," http://www.myriobiblos.gr/texts/english/economou_ecology_1.html.

Ecumenical Patriarch on environmental issues, has noted that, "In his now classic article entitled 'The Roots of our Ecological Crisis,' Lynn White already suspected—although he did not elaborate on—the truth behind asceticism."[15] Furthermore, Orthodox theologian Elizabeth Theokritoff has pointed out the beneficial effects of Orthodox fasting discipline (which includes abstaining from sexual relations) on population control.[16] Given

---

[15] John Chryssavgis, "A New Heaven and a New Earth: Orthodox Theology and an Ecological World View," *The Ecumenical Review* 62, no. 2 (2010): 214–22. As we noted above (see chap. 3, "Humanity's Place in Creation—Microcosm," n. 17, 40), White's article is notable for its erroneous portrayal of Christian thinking (of either Western or Eastern perspectives). Chryssavgis' favorable mention of it is deeply disturbing.

[16] Elizabeth Theokritoff, "A Eucharistic and Ascetic Ethos: Orthodox Christianity and the Environment," *Shap Journal* 31 (2008–2009), http://www.shapworkingparty.org.uk/journals/articles_0809/ theokritoff. The fixation of environmentalists on population control represents another area in which Christian thinking differs significantly from the tenets of modern environmental religion. This is a subject that we hope to explore in depth in later work, but for now we note that we believe the Christian view of humankind is more in keeping with economist Julian Simon's emphasis on the potential of each person to be a source of creativity—the "ultimate resource" in Simon's phrasing:

> If humankind did not have a propensity to create more than it uses, the species would have perished a long time ago. This propensity to build may be taken as a fundamental characteristic that is part of our evolution. This is the overarching theory that explains why events turn out in exactly the opposite fashion from what Malthus and his followers foresaw.

See Julian Simon, *The Ultimate Resource 2* (Princeton: University Press 1996), 582.

the temptation to which many have succumbed, a few words on the proper role of asceticism are in order.

Asceticism comes from the Greek *askēsis*, which simply means "exercise." Asceticism, therefore, is simply spiritual exercise undertaken for the health of the soul. Here, we must be careful to set aside popular caricatures of asceticism as either a kind of masochistic, self-flagellated misery or a kind of Gnostic attitude which exalts lofty spiritual things over crass material things.[17] (This latter view is often associated with those environmentalists who have constructed a religion of nature worship.)[18] It is

---

[17] Orthodox asceticism must also be distinguished from Western, especially Roman Catholic, notions of penance or penitential discipline and satisfaction for sins. With regard to the caricature of asceticism, Fr. Dumitru Stăniloae notes,

> According to the current use of the word, asceticism has a negative connotation. It means a negative holding back, a negative restraint, or a negative effort. This is because the sinful tendencies of our nature, the habitual things that lead to its death, have come to be considered as the positive side of life. Ascetical striving, though negative in appearance, confronts the negative element in human nature with the intent to eliminate it by permanent opposition.

Orthodox Spirituality (South Canaan, PA: St. Tikhon's Seminary Press, 2002), 25.

[18] Deep ecologists "seek the healing of alienation from self, community, and the Earth that shallow ecology has caused." Philip F. Cramer, *Deep Environmental Politics: The Role of Radical Environmentalism in Crafting American Environmental Policy* (Westport, CT: Praeger Publishing, 1998), 4. "But there's something more going on with environmentalism … [with the idea that] environmentalism really does involve a form of spiritualism or worship. The graven idol, in this case, is nature itself. Deep ecology is what people have in mind." David Roberts, "Environmentalism as a Religion: What Does the Accusation Mean and How Should Greens Respond?"

neither. Rather, asceticism is a positive, life-affirming attitude and set of practices that seeks human freedom by overcoming the *passions*—the sinful and disordered habits and attitudes that poison our relationships, primarily with God but also with ourselves, our neighbor, and the world. These passions are the "seven deadly sins" of classical spirituality that enslave the heart, cloud the reason, poison relationships, and in general lead to the disintegration and corruption of the soul,[19] and by extension, to the misery of the world caused by corrupted people acting in corrupted ways.

Much could be said about asceticism and the passions, but for our purposes, we might say that to be ascetic is to learn to live rightly on the earth with God, our neighbor, and creation. With regard to our relationships, our ascetic stance before God is one of humility and obedience. Before our neighbor, as the gospel puts it, we seek to be the last, not the first; humbled, not exalted; the servant, not the master.[20] Before creation, "Man dies as to his claim to be God in creation, and instead recognizes God as its Lord."[21] In each case, we are brought to a new relationship with the other; in the case of our relationship to

---

Grist, August 10, 2005, http://grist.org/article/environmentalism-as-a-religion/. Quoting writer and conservationist Michael Frome, "We need a community of faith—faith in nature, in humankind, and in each other," see Philip Shabecoff, *Earth Rising: American Environmentalism in the 21st Century* (Washington, DC: Island Press, 2000), 76.

[19] The classical list of the seven deadly sins in the West includes: lust, gluttony, avarice, discouragement/sloth, anger, envy, and pride. In the Eastern Church, the passions traditionally number eight and are usually listed in the order Evagrius gives them: gluttony, fornication, avarice, grief, wrath, listlessness, vainglory, and pride.

[20] See Mark 10:13; Matthew 23:12; Mark 10:43.

[21] John Zizioulas, "Proprietors or Priests of Creation?" chapter 7 in *The Eucharistic Communion and the World*, ed. Luke Ben Tallon

creation, an ascetical stance clearly alters the demands we make on the material world, both *what* we ask of it and *how much* we ask. In this respect, Orthodoxy's call to ascetic striving for the sake of one's salvation is in line with free market principles of *voluntary* activity and lifestyle choices.

The ascetical tradition of the Orthodox Church includes many practices: prayer, fasting, almsgiving, keeping vigil, *inter alia*. They are the active part of the spiritual life, our voluntary cooperation with the grace of God. As such, it is important that we not be tempted to use the ascetical practices of the Church for ends they were not designed to serve. Thus, we need to be careful of "environmental consciousness" masquerading as authentic spiritual practice. Moreover, we must keep in mind that it is the believer's *practice* of asceticism, not asceticism *qua* asceticism, that is important.

For example, fasting out of ecological conviction, or eating "lower on the food chain"[22] (i.e., avoiding meat or eating a vegan diet) is spiritually useless for the Christian. Fasting is not dieting; neither is it an ecological statement. For a Christian, fasting is a spiritual discipline that is fruitful when it is joined with prayer and repentance, a discipline that is oriented toward God to effect the purification and transfiguration of the heart. What is more, for Orthodox Christians to use the ascetical discipline of fasting for any other purpose *undermines* its real purpose. If we do not use ascetical disciplines to grow in a right relationship with God, we will not grow in right relationships with

---

(London: T&T Clark, 1988), 138, http://www.resourcesforchristiantheology.org/?p=124.

[22] Frederick Krueger, "Guidelines for the Greening of the Orthodox Parish," http://orth-transfiguration.org/library/orthodoxy/guidelines/ (accessed June 22, 2010, no longer available). It may also be useless for the environment. See Pierre Desrochers and Hiroko Shimizu, *The Locovore's Dilemma: In Praise of the 10,000 Mile Diet* (New York, NY: PublicAffairs, 2012).

our neighbor or with creation either.[23] This leads us to a deep irony that seems to be lost on those who focus on the superficial similarities between Christian asceticism and environmentalists' calls for restricting consumption: *concern for the environment that distracts us from the purification and illumination of the heart will actually hinder our ability to transfigure creation and offer it back to Christ.* That is to say, *concern for environmentalism is inversely proportional to our effectiveness in transfiguring the environment.* At this point, we are tempted to leave off writing altogether, lest our efforts undermine the end we are trying to pursue. Having drawn attention to the danger and the temptation, however, we can proceed if we do so with caution.

In short, spiritual tools must be used for spiritual ends. We "seek first his kingdom and his righteousness, and all these things shall be yours as well" (Matt. 6:33). As Elizabeth Theokritoff reminds us,

> The salvation of the earth is not in our hands, either individually or as a human collective: it is the work of the Creator and Saviour, and our task is to conform ourselves to him. Re-created in the image of the new Adam, we are called to image God's love and compassion for all creation, so fulfilling his economy of salvation by growing into his likeness.[24]

What then is the Christian to do to integrate the Church's ascetical traditions into his or her interactions with God's cre-

---

[23] *Pace*, for example, John Chryssavgis's description of fasting in "Icons, Liturgy, Saints: Ecological Insights from Orthodox Spirituality," *International Review of Missions* 99, no. 2 (2010): 187–88.

[24] Elizabeth Theokritoff, "The Salvation of the World and Saving the Earth: An Orthodox Christian Approach," *Worldviews* 14 (2010): 141-56, 155. See also the *Bases of the Social Concept*, 13.5.3, "It is impossible to overcome the ecological crisis in the situation of a spiritual crisis."

ation? First, we must resist the temptation to impose our asceticism on others, as the value of the ascetical practices lie in the *voluntary* denial of consumption as a means of growing closer to God. Using the power of the state to compel asceticism in others would thus be counterproductive in a spiritual sense. Moreover, we must distinguish our own practice of asceticism from efforts to deny others' the benefits of God-given human creativity; we cannot force asceticism onto others. For example, efforts to restrict the increasing use of energy by the world's poor are at odds both with true asceticism and with our duty to be charitable to our neighbors. Given the horrific costs of indoor air pollution caused by burning dung and similar fuels in homes by the world's poorest, building electrical power plants in poor countries should be applauded.[25]

Second, we must also avoid shifting the costs and burdens of our own "asceticism" onto others. Lobbying for subsidies and mandates for corn-based ethanol that leads to higher food prices, at tremendous cost to the world's poor, is a particularly pernicious example of faux asceticism in which the warm feelings of doing good among the wealthy are primarily paid for by the poorest. For example, a Tufts University study estimated that US corn ethanol mandates cost Mexico $1.5 to $3 billion through increased food prices from 2006 to 2011. Similarly, the European Union's Common Agricultural Policy imposes tremendous costs on the poor in developing countries by denying them markets for their agricultural products through subsidies to European farmers in the name of promoting sustainable agriculture.[26]

---

[25] Andrew Morriss and Roger E. Meiners, "Borders and the Environment," *Environmental Law* 39 (2009): 141.

[26] Timothy A. Wise, *The Cost to Mexico of U.S. Corn Ethanol Expansion* (Tufts Global Development and Environment Institute, May 2012), http://www.ase.tufts.edu/gdae/Pubs/wp/12-01WiseBiofuels.pdf; Ann-Christina L. Knudsen, *Farmers on Welfare: The Making of*

Third, we must resist the temptation to seek to subsidize our own consumption. If doctors are enjoined to "first, do no harm," a similar injunction applies to government policies. Providing ourselves with subsidized goods and services, such as fuels, food, and electricity, not only encourages overconsumption of those goods and services, thus leading us away from both good stewardship and opportunities to practice asceticism, but also causes damage to God's creation. The vast, federally subsidized water projects in the western United States and the World Bank's tragic record of supporting destructive "infrastructure" projects such as dams in developing countries are two examples.[27] No less damaging is the common practice in oil-producing nations of subsidizing consumption of fossil fuels—Venezuela's $0.04 per gallon gasoline is similarly a destructive practice. In each case, creation is sacrificed to venal goals—such as purchasing voters' support for governments—that are inconsistent with our responsibility as stewards.

Three Ways of Living in the Creation

We suggest that there are three ways of relating to God that, by extension, point to ways of relating to our neighbor and to the

---

Europe's Common Agricultural Policy (New York: Cornell University Press, 2009); Andrew Schmitz et al., *Agricultural Policy, Agribusiness, and Rent-Seeking Behaviour* (Toronto: University of Toronto Press, 2010).

[27] Marc Reisner, *Cadillac Desert: The American West and Its Disappearing Water* (New York: Penguin Books, 1993); Phillippe Le Pestre, *The World Bank and the Environmental Challenge* (Susquehanna, PA: Susquehanna University Press, 1989); Andrew C. Revkin, "World Bank Criticized on Environmental Efforts," *N.Y. Times* July 22, 2008, http://www.nytimes.com/2008/07/22/science/earth/23enviro.html?_r=0.

world. The illustration is taken from St. Basil the Great, but it is found in several other Fathers as well.[28] Basil says,

> In all, I observe three different dispositions which lead invariably to obedience: either we turn aside from evil from the fear of punishment and so are in a servile disposition; or, seeking the profits of a wage, we fulfill what is enjoined for the sake of our own profit and are therefore like mercenaries; or else we do so for the good itself and for love of him who gave us the law, rejoicing to be thought worthy of serving so glorious and good a God, in which case we are surely in the disposition of sons.[29]

---

[28] See, for example, the *Holy Rule* of St. Benedict, chap. 7, on the movement from fear to love; St. John Cassian, *Institutes* 4.39 and *Conferences* 11.6–7; St. Dorotheus of Gaza, *Discourse 4, On the Fear of God* (Cistercian Studies 33 [Kalamazoo, MI: Cistercian Publications, 1978], 110) and *Directions on Spiritual Life*, 23. St. John Climacus, *Ladder of Divine Ascent* 1.13 (Boston, MA: Holy Transfiguration Monastery, 1978), 7, has a particularly nice variation:

> The man who renounces the world *from fear* is like burning incense that begins with fragrance but ends in smoke. He who leaves the world *through hope of reward* is like a millstone that always moves in the same way [i.e., round and round in a circle]. But he who withdraws from the world *out of love for God* has obtained fire at the very outset; and, like fire set to fuel, it soon kindles a larger fire" [emphasis added].

A further analogy might possibly be found in St. Paul's distinction between the *sarkikos* (carnal), *psychikos* (often translated "natural," but more accurately psychical or psychological), and *pneumatikos* (spiritual) man in 1 Corinthians 2:14–3:3; but this is a line of inquiry is outside the scope of this study.

[29] Prologue to the *Longer Responses, The Asketikon of St. Basil the Great*, trans. and ed. Anna Silvas, Oxford Early Christian Studies (Oxford: Oxford University Press, 2007), 156–57 (PG 31.896B2-12).

Therefore the three dispositions are those of a slave, a servant, and a son.

Slave

A *slave* obeys the Father out of fear of punishment or out of fear of hell. The analog among environmentalists is the fear-mongering language of crisis, catastrophe, apocalypse, global disaster, total destruction, cataclysm, and so forth, of which we often read. For example, Paul Ehrlich, beginning with *The Population Bomb* in 1968, has built a long career out of predicting environmental disasters (which never arrive). The contemporary Greek theologian Metropolitan John (Zizioulas) of Pergamon has recognized this tendency in some of the environmental literature and has spoken to it (though he himself is also guilty of it at times, as are many other Orthodox writers).[30]

We acknowledge that fear can be a powerful incentive for action, but actions based on fear, because they are founded on emotion and not on clear reasoning, tend toward the irrational and are therefore untrustworthy. We prefer that our witness not

---

[30] He speaks against it in "Ecological Asceticism: A Cultural Revolution," *Our Planet* 7.6 (April 1996), http://www.orthodoxresearchinstitute.org/articles/misc/john_zizoulias_ecological_asceticism.htm, but falls victim to it in "The Theological Approach to the Environmental Problem," http://www.rsesymposia.org/more.php?&pcatid=45&theitemid=56&catid=161. Likewise Patriarch Bartholomew I of Constantinople spoke against it, "Message on the Day of Prayer for Creation, 1 September 1993," http://www.patriarchate.org/documents/1993-encyclical, but seems to have given in to it more recently, for example, "Message on the Day of Prayer for Creation, 1 September 2006," http://www.patriarchate.org/documents/2006-encyclical, and "Opening Address of His All Holiness Ecumenical Patriarch Bartholomew at the 8th RSE Symposium, October 21, 2009," http://www.patriarchate.org/documents/2009-rse-patriarch-opening.

be a slavish one, borne out of fear, but a hopeful one grounded in a better rationale. The Orthodox should therefore reject the tendency toward apocalyptic rhetoric among many environmentalists.[31]

Servant

A more hopeful disposition can be found in that of a *servant* who obeys the Father out of a desire for reward—the reward of heaven—or, more immanently, for a better world, cleaner air and water, and a cleaner conscience. Here, a great deal of work has been done by Christian environmentalists who have developed and promoted *stewardship* as the model of Christian care for the world.[32] The literature on stewardship is vast,[33] and

---

[31] M. Jimmie Killingsworth and Jacqueline S. Palmer, "Millennial Ecology: The Apocalyptic Narrative from *Silent Spring* to Global Warming," in *Green Culture: Environmental Rhetoric in Contemporary America*, ed. Carl G. Herndl and Stuart C. Brown, (Madison, WI: University of Wisconsin Press, 1996), 21.

[32] The idea of stewardship is found often in the Fathers. See, for example, St. Basil the Great, *Sermon 7, To the Rich* 3 (PG 31.288B2), *Sermon 6, "I will tear down my barns,"* 2, 7 (PG 31.264C11, 276B4-77A8), both of which can be found in C. Paul Schroeder, trans. *On Social Justice: St. Basil the Great* (Crestwood, NY: St. Vladimir's Seminary Press, 2009), 46, 61–62, 69–70, respectively. Also, St. John Chrysostom, *On Lazarus* 2.5 (PG 48.988), in *St. John Chrysostom, On Wealth and Poverty* (Crestwood, NY: St. Vladimir's Seminary Press, 1984), 50; idem., *On Genesis* 35.8 (PG 55.331-32), idem., *On First Corinthians* 10.3 (PG 61.85-86); and St. Symeon the New Theologian, *Catechetical Orations* 9. See Keselopoulos, *Man and the Environment*, n. 81, 127. See also the *Bases of the Social Concept*, 13.2.

[33] See, for example and a good place to begin, the resources available at http://www.acton.org/public-policy/environmental-stewardship.

there is much in the stewardship model that we find positive and helpful.

Perhaps the paradigmatic example of the opportunity for good stewardship is the rancher or farmer who directly cares for the land. Such stewardship depends on local knowledge, the knowledge of time and place that only someone intimately familiar with a particular corner of God's creation can possess. This is a calling to the farmer or rancher as a person to conduct himself or herself in a fashion that will bring God's praise as a "good and faithful servant," not a call for centralized management by bureaucracies. The call to stewardship is not limited to those in agriculture, however. It is a call to us all. Each of us has numerous opportunities in our daily lives to demonstrate good stewardship, whether by small acts, such as retrieving a piece of litter on a walk, to larger acts of caring for the resources given into our custody. Good stewardship may be as simple as following manufacturer's directions when fertilizing our lawns to making the effort to prevent waste by fixing a leaky faucet. Again, the focus is properly on the person, whose conduct must be judged by the circumstances in which the person finds himself or herself. Thus Rachel Carson properly denounced the US government's mass spraying campaigns against gypsy moths, which indiscriminately blanketed the land with DDT, but those who came after her and broadly campaigned against DDT inappropriately failed to take into account the vital role of the indoor spraying of DDT in malarial areas and how banning DDT in those areas contributed to the illnesses and deaths of millions.[34]

---

[34] Donald Roberts and Richard Tren, "Did Rachel Carson Understand the Importance of DDT in Global Public Health Programs?" in *Silent Spring at 50: The False Crises of Rachel Carson*, ed. Roger Meiners, Pierre Desrochers, and Andrew Morriss (Washington, DC: Cato Institute, 2012): 167–99; Donald Roberts and Richard

However, the disposition of a servant, while certainly better than that of a slave, is not ultimately the best one (we still have to speak of the disposition of a son). A servant, and the stewardship model, work out of a master/servant relationship, and seems to imply a managerial approach to creation, one in which humanity is set over and above the creation and relates to it in an external way.[35] It does not require, for example, seeing beyond the outward appearances of things to discerning their *logoi* and how each of those *logoi* are related to the whole creation and to the *Logos* himself. It does not require that we see man as the microcosm of creation, and it is far from the notion that creation is a part of mankind. Thus, in the Orthodox view, our relationship to the environment is not an external relationship; rather, it is an internal one, constituent of who we are, ontological

---

Tren, *The Excellent Powder: DDT's Political and Scientific History* (Indianapolis, IN: Dog Ear Publishing, 2010). On the mass spraying campaigns and pesticide issues, see Andrew Morriss and Roger E. Meiners, "Market Principles for Pesticides," *William & Mary Environmental Law & Policy Review* 28, no. 1 (2003): 35–86; and Andrew Morriss and Roger E. Meiners, "Property Rights, Pesticides and Public Health: Explaining the Paradox of Modern Pesticide Policy," *Fordham Environmental Law Journal* 14 (2002): 1–53.

[35] John Zizioulas's brief critique of the stewardship model can be found in "Proprietors or Priests of Creation?" chapter 7 in *The Eucharistic Communion and the World*, ed. Luke Ben Tallon (London: T&T Clark, 2011), http://stpaulsirvine.org/html/proprietororpriest.htm. See also John Zizioulas, opening plenary address, "Towards an Environmental Ethic," *Religion, Science and the Environment Symposium IV. The Adriatic Sea: A Sea at Risk, a Unity of Purpose, 6 June 2002*, http://www.rsesymposia.org/themedia/File/1151678281-Ethic.pdf. See also *Bases of the Social Concept*, 13.5.2, the environment is "no longer perceived as home and all the more so as temple, becoming only 'habitat.'"

even. In light of this view, the disposition of a servant and the stewardship model fall a little short.[36]

To anticipate our later discussion on the human role as priest of creation, Zizioulas draws out some of the implications of the stewardship model for us:

> The understanding of the human being as priest rather than steward of creation means that the role of man in creation is neither passive (conservationist) nor managerial, *i.e.* "economic".… The human being is related to nature not *functionally*, as the idea of stewardship would suggest, but *ontologically*: *by being the steward of creation the human being relates to nature by what he does, whereas by being the priest of creation he relates to nature by what he is*.… Ecology is in this way a matter of our *esse*, not of our *bene esse*. Our ecological concern becomes in this way far more powerful and efficient than in employing the model of stewardship.[37]

Granting all the good that the stewardship model offers us, we would like to propose that there is still "a more excellent way."

Son

The best disposition is that of a *son*, modeled for us by Christ himself, who obeys the Father simply out of love for the Father. It is true that "The earth is the LORD's and the fulness thereof, the world and those who dwell therein" (Ps. 24:1), but it is also true that the Lord, out of his love for mankind, has given everything to us: "all that is mine is yours" (Luke 15:31), says the Father to the elder brother in the parable of the prodigal

---

[36] Vigen Guroian, "Ecological Ethics," 159–60, offers further Orthodox critique of the stewardship model.

[37] John Zizioulas, "Proprietors or Priests of Creation?" iv.1. Emphasis added.

son. We, in imitation of the Father who gives everything to us, return everything to the Father in thanksgiving and love. This is a liturgical function, and it underscores the importance of an ecclesial response to ecological issues.

The closer we approach the status of sons, the greater our intimacy with God. The more intimate we are with God, the greater our sanctification and the more we are healed of sin and the corrupting effect of the passions. When the microcosm (man) is healed, the macrocosm (creation) will be healed as well, for the state of the macrocosm reveals the state of the microcosm.[38] This is why it is important that the ascetical practices of the Church not be diverted to any other purpose than the sanctification of mankind: They serve the environment best when they serve our sanctification most.

Status of Sons

How shall we flesh out a son's relationship with the Father? We suggest that we look to Christ and to his work, in particular to his traditionally acknowledged roles of king, prophet, and priest.[39]

---

[38] In this context, the famous statement of St. Seraphim of Sarov becomes clear: "Acquire the Spirit of peace, and a thousand souls around you will be saved." Also, St. Isaac the Syrian, "Be at peace with your own soul; then heaven and earth will be at peace with you." As Aidan Hart, "The Pain of the Earth," notes, "If modern man is not at peace with the earth it is because he is not at peace with himself and God."

[39] Aidan Hart also finds the classical offices of Christ as king, prophet, and priest a helpful organizing principle. See his article, "Transfiguring Matter: Icons as a Paradigm for Christian Ecology," http://aidanharticons.com/wp-content/uploads/2012/08/ICON-ECOL.pdf. Fr. Dumitru Stăniloae did too. See Radu Bordeianu, "Priesthood Natural, Universal and Ordained: Dumitru Stăniloae's Communion Ecclesiology," *Pro Ecclesia* 19, no. 4 (2010): 405–33.

King

St. Gregory the Theologian says that Adam was "king of all upon earth, but subject to the King above."[40] Adam's kingship is tied to the notion of *dominion*, which was given in the first chapter of Genesis, "Be fruitful and multiply, and fill the earth and subdue it; and have dominion over the fish of the sea and over the birds of the air and over every living thing that moves upon the earth" (Gen. 1:28). Some have blamed Christianity; as we noted earlier, chief among them was medieval historian Lynn T. White, Jr. in his 1967 article, "The Historical Roots of Our Ecological Crisis,"[41] which many credit with a key role in launching the modern environmental movement. In particular, White attacked Christianity's notion of dominion over creation as a major cause of modern ecological problems.[42] As the Baptist scholar Ben Philips notes,

---

[40] *Oration 38, On the Theophany*, 11 (PG 36.324A4), http://www.newadvent.org/fathers/310238.htm.

[41] *Science* 155 (March, 1967): 1203–7.

[42] Regrettably, a few Orthodox theologians have uncritically accepted his thesis, for example, John D. Zizioulas, noted earlier (see chap. 4, "Living in the Creation: An Orthodox Ethos," n. 15, 54), who says, "The American historian Lynn White was right to attribute the causes of the [ecological] problem to Christian theology, particularly of the Western Church, which exploited the verses of Genesis containing God's order to the first human beings to 'dominate the earth' in order to encourage them, as Descartes bluntly put it, to be 'masters and possessors of nature.'" "Ecological Asceticism: A Cultural Revolution," http://www.orthodoxresearchinstitute.org/articles/misc/john_zizoulias_ecological_asceticism.htm. See also, John D. Zizioulas, "Preserving God's Creation: Three Lectures on Theology and Ecology," *King's Theological Review*, 12, no. 1 (1989): 1–5, and "The Theological Approach to the Ecological Problem," http://www.rsesymposia.org/more.php?&pcatid=45&theitemid=56&catid=161. See also,

The basic argument linking tyranny over and exploitation of nature with Christianity may be identified as the "mastery hypothesis." The argument is generally made along three major lines: Christianity is said to have killed off humanity's wonder and awe of nature by de-sacralizing nature, it promotes an anthropocentrism which legitimates human rule and dominion over nature, and it relegates the physical world to a lower status and value than that which is spirit.[43]

We will not enter into a general defense of the dominion mandate here,[44] but we do suggest that there are ways of affirming it that avoid some of the negative connotations it raises for some people. For example, the *Bases of the Social Concept* says,

> "Dominion" over nature and "subjection" of the earth (Gen. 1:28), to which man is called, do not mean all-permissiveness in God's design. It only means that man is the bearer of the image of the heavenly Housekeeper and as such should express, according to St. Gregory of Nyssa, his royal dignity not in dominion over the world

---

Christos Yannaras, "Ecology by Process of Elimination … and Christmas," http://www.oodegr.com/english/koinwnia/perivallon/eis_atopon1.htm.

[43] Benjamin B. Philips, "A Creature among Creatures or Lords of Creation? The Vocation of Dominion in Christian Theology," *Journal of Markets & Morality* 14, no. 1 (2011): 133. Alas, John Zizioulas seems to have accepted all three of these criticisms of Christianity, along with some unfortunate misapprehensions of Western (especially American) history. See his "Orthodoxy and Ecological Problems: A Theological Approach," http://www.orthodoxresearchinstitute.org/articles/misc/john_pergamon_ecological_problems.htm.

[44] Benjamin B. Philips' paper (n. 43 *supra*) would be a good place to start.

around him or violence towards it, but in "dressing" and "keeping" the magnificent kingdom of nature for which he is responsible before God.[45]

Similarly Aidan Hart speaks of "artistic skillfulness," that kind of love and respect that a master craftsman brings to his work, which "entails a sympathy with the materials, a desire to bring the best out of them, to discover and bring to fruition the inner essence of each material." Here we can think of a cabinetmaker respecting the grain of wood or of a soprano singing her aria.

> The craftsman raises his material to a higher plane by, as it were, mingling it with his intelligence—and of course by contrast a poor workman will debase his material by mingling it with his ineptitude. Surely it is as a skilled artist and craftsman that man is called to exercise his dominion—to mingle it with his spirit, and through him, to mingle it with God's Spirit, to sublimate it, to transfigure it; not to enslave creation but to save it.[46]

Beyond simple ineptitude there is, of course, the near certainty of human sin marring creation. The likelihood of our corrupting the world is all the greater because we are happy to remember that we are "king of all upon earth," but we tend to forget that we are, at the same time, "subject to the King above." This means just as creation is subject to *our* dominion over *it*, we are subject to *God's* dominion over *us*.

However, more than that, because we are "earthly and heavenly, temporal and yet immortal, visible and yet intellectual, half-way between greatness and lowliness, in one person combining spirit and flesh,"[47] we stand not only as microcosms of

---

[45] *Bases of the Social Concept*, 13.2.

[46] Aidan Hart, "Icons and Transfiguring Matter," 5.

[47] This is the continuation of the quotation from St. Gregory the Theologian, *Oration* 30, *On the Theophany*, 11, above (PG 36.324A4-7).

the cosmos, but also as mediators of the creation to the Creator. It is our role, as kings of creation, not simply to dominate or administer the created order on our own, by our own devices and for our own ends, but to dominate and order the world by uniting it with God. Only in union with God can the right ordering of the world be accomplished. Christ himself did this work of recapitulation through his incarnation and the cosmic task of mediating the five distinctions we outlined above.

Humanity is able to mediate this union because our unique position in the world is precisely that of microcosm. We are the only creatures who are composite beings, made up of body and rational soul, being "earthly and heavenly, temporal and yet immortal," and thus we are the only creatures who are able to transcend the world while being fully part of it. If we are to effect the union of creation with God, we ourselves need to be united with God. Thus we underscore again the place of Christian observance and asceticism in the life of the one who would be king.

Practically speaking, God has entrusted to us many special places of great natural beauty, which we have within our power to preserve or to sacrifice to other goals. We must use great caution in exercising our dominion over nature in making such choices. We can thus join with John Muir (d. 1914) in his anguished cry over the damming of the Hetch Hetchy Valley: "Dam Hetch Hetchy! As well dam for water-tanks the people's cathedrals and churches, for no holier temple has ever been consecrated by the heart of man."[48] However unlike Muir and many other environmentalists, we recognize that many development projects that alter the environment are essential to the human flourishing that our Father wishes for us.

---

[48] John Muir, *The Yosemite* (New York: Century, 1912), 262. Available in Roderick Nash, *The American Environment: Readings in The History of Conservation* (Reading, Mass.: Addison-Wesley, 1968).

Prophet

The prophetic role is closely tied to natural contemplation. We have spoken to the importance of asceticism in moral formation and the cultivation of virtue. Natural contemplation is necessarily founded on the basis of ascetical effort undertaken in the practical life. In fact, there is clear danger in neglecting moral formation in virtue:

> We should abstain from natural contemplation until we are fully prepared [through asceticism and cultivation of virtue], lest in trying to perceive the spiritual essences [*logoi*] of visible creatures we reap passions by mistake. For the outward forms of visible things have greater power over the senses of those who are immature than the essences [*logoi*] hidden in the forms of things have over their souls.[49]

The danger, then, is with immature persons who are easily distracted by their senses that lead them into passions—avarice, lust, anger, and the like—and from there into a passionate use of others and the world to satisfy their disordered desires. This is the exact situation that gives rise to abuses of our neighbor and of the rest of creation; it is the fallen state of mankind. The active practice of asceticism and the cultivation of the virtues are therefore necessary in and of themselves, not only as a restraint on the passions and the disciplined effort of uprooting them and their pernicious effects, but also because asceticism

---

[49] St. Maximus the Confessor, *Centuries on Various Texts* 2.85, Philokalia 2.205. Recall, too, the passage from *Questions to Thalassius* 32 quoted above: "If someone mingles and confuses the letter of the [scripture], the outward appearance of visible things, and his own sense with one another, he 'is blind and short-sighted' (2 Peter 1:9) and suffers from ignorance of the true Cause of created beings."

blossoms into contemplation. The state of contemplation is one of dispassion (Gk. *apatheia*), a state not of apathy, as the Greek term might imply, but rather one of interior freedom, the calm of detachment, in which the passions are quieted and no longer have free reign in the soul, and inner freedom opens up the possibility of loving God, neighbor, and creation in a respectful, nonpossessive way, dispassionately or disinterestedly.

Moreover, this helps guide us in understanding how we are to act to care for God's creation. In many cases, a need is readily identified but we face a choice across a wide range of possible remedies for addressing the problem. A proper understanding of the fallen nature of man and our need to cultivate the virtues can help guide us in selecting the appropriate means. For example, man's fallen nature should make us wary of centralizing power in the hands of government officials who are not exempt from that fallen nature. Giving officials' discretionary power over others' activities, for example, through requiring permits and licenses, can risk the corruption of that man's fallen nature. The recent revelations of mass official corruption in the Greek government, from the consistent demand for bribes to the failure of officials to pay the taxes they demand of others, are just particularly extreme examples of how a state-centered society can fail by centralizing its power. In the case of environmental regulation, not only do prescriptive "command and control" regulations risk encouraging such behavior by creating occasions of sin, but they also deny individuals the opportunity to develop their own virtuous behavior through contemplation and action. As James Madison observed,

> If men were angels, no government would be necessary. If angels were to govern men, neither external nor internal controls on government would be necessary. In framing a government which is to be administered by men over men, the great difficulty lies in this: you must first enable

the government to control the governed; and in the next place oblige it to control itself. A dependence on the people is, no doubt, the primary control on the government; but experience has taught mankind the necessity of auxiliary precautions."[50]

This wisdom is consistent with Orthodox teachings on the fallen nature of man and cautions us to focus our attention on both halves of Madison's formula—the control of the government as well as the control of the governed. There are no doubt instances when direct government action is necessary in the care of creation, but we must remember that the details of the institutions we design for the care of creation will be operated by men, not by angels. We are not suggesting, of course, that God has an opinion on the rightness or wrongness of particular legislation. Rather, we believe that he calls us to use our God-given wisdom to make intelligent decisions about both our own actions and the institutions we design to govern our societies. Good use of our talents involves both.

To return to our analysis, contemplation consists of two stages. The latter stage and ultimate aim of contemplation is union with God through pure prayer, but the earlier stage of contemplation is to come to knowledge of creatures through the contemplation of their nature (*theoria physikē*). Such natural contemplation consists in perceiving the *logoi* of things. The "contemplation of the logoi in creation (*theōria physikē*) belongs to the work of the Spirit in man's sanctification and deification.

---

[50] James Madison, "Federalist, no. 51," in *The Federalist*, ed. George W. Carey and James McClellan (Indianapolis: Liberty Fund, 2001), 269, http://oll.libertyfund.org/?option=com_staticxt&staticfile=show. php%3Ftitle=788&chapter=108659&layout=html&Itemid=27.

This intellectual process is not separated from spiritual growth but is an integral part of it."[51]

The *logos* of a thing, the *logos* of its nature (*logos physeos*), as we have seen, is the presence of the divine wisdom, the Word of God, in created things. As such, it cannot be corrupted by the fall (otherwise it would cease to be what it is). However, the *way* in which a particular thing (or person) lives out that *logos* is subject to variation, and given the fall, the manner or mode of existence (*tropos hyparxeos*) for creatures is unstable, disordered, and corrupted. The practical life of asceticism is, functionally, the stabilization and reintegration of a person's life according to God's intention for him or her, that is, according to his or her own *logos*. Once this stability and reintegration begins to be manifest, natural contemplation becomes possible.

Natural contemplation fulfills man's prophetic role by revealing to him the purpose of God in created things through the recognition of their *logoi*. It requires the attentiveness of dispassion so that the mind, stripped free of covetousness and all passions, is able to see things not simply as they are (or, worse, as we want them to be) but as God intends them to be. This recognition of *logoi*, which begins in a scientific (*epistēmonikōs*) investigation of the phenomenal world, matures in its latter stages into an intuitive grasp of the inner principles of things and ultimately of their unity in the one Logos of God. That is, natural contemplation proceeds from seeing God in creation to seeing creation in God.

What might the latter stages of natural contemplation look like? An incident from the life of St. Benedict of Nursia (d. 547), the founder of the Benedictine order, can provide an illustration:

> While the disciples were still sleeping, Benedict the man
> of God was already keeping vigil, anticipating the hour

---

[51] Thunberg, *Microcosm and Mediator*, 82.

of the night office. Standing in front of his window in the dead of night he was praying to the Lord Almighty when suddenly he saw a light shining.... As he described it later, the whole world was gathered up before his eyes as if in a ray of sunlight.... How is it possible for the whole world to be seen in this way by a human being?... The soul of the contemplative transcends itself when, in God's light, it is transported beyond itself. Then, looking below itself, it understands how limited is that which on earth seemed to it to have no limits.... When it is said that the world was gathered up before his eyes that does not mean that heaven and earth were contracted. No. The soul of the seer was expanded. Enraptured with God he was able to see without difficulty everything that is under God.[52]

Thus, while natural contemplation begins with scientific investigation and discursive reason, it proceeds to a more immediate (that is, *unmediated*) apprehension or intuition. "The Christian contemplates creation as it were from above, or from within, and not through its external sensible impressions."[53] By discerning the *logoi* of things, a person is better able to see how to use the things of the world in accordance with the purpose God intended for them. As Stăniloae says, "The world is a teacher to lead us to Christ. Of course it can also be the road to hell. It is the tree of the knowledge of good and evil, the tree of testing. If we look at its beauty in order to praise its Creator, we are saved; if we think that its fruit is pure and simply something to eat, we

---

[52] Pope St. Gregory the Great (d. 604), *Dialogues* 2.35 (PL 66.198-200), quoted in Olivier Clément, *The Roots of Christian Mysticism: Texts from the Patristic Era with Commentary*, trans. Theodore Berkeley and Jeremy Hummerstone (Hyde Park, NY: New City Press, 1993), 225–26.

[53] Thunberg, *Man and Cosmos*, 136.

are lost."[54] To the degree that progress in natural contemplation involves increasing degrees of intuition, it is difficult to say more about it, and we are happy to cede the discussion to those who have greater experience in it than we do.

We should offer two caveats. First, there is no basis for assuming that God's intention for a mountain full of coal, for example, precludes the mining of that coal. Natural contemplation is not a bucolic stroll through the mountains, admiring what God hath wrought. It is a rigorous, dispassionate investigation of the *logoi* inherent in the mountain, including the *logos* of the coal in it. Consider, for example, that an estimated 1.5 billion people today lack access to electricity around the world.[55] Access to electricity is positively associated with increases in the Human Development Index.[56] While coal has some disadvantages as a fuel for power generation, many of these can be mitigated by existing technologies. Moreover, it is widely available, inexpensive, and easy to use. Its use in central power generation facilities is far less damaging to human health and the environment than its direct use in homes because emissions can be more cost effectively addressed on a larger scale. We believe a Christian response to the poverty of this 1.5 billion should include both the environmental costs of developing coal resources and the human costs of not doing so. We believe the most likely result of such an analysis will be the conclusion that in some instances developing the resources are justified and in some instances, they are not.

---

[54] Stăniloae, *Orthodox Spirituality*, 205.

[55] World Health Organization and UNDEP, *The Energy Access Situation in Developing Countries* 1 (2009).

[56] Alan D. Pasternak, "Global Energy Futures and Human Development: A Framework for Analysis" (2000), https://e-reports-ext.llnl.gov/pdf/239193.pdf.

Second, when discussing natural contemplation, we are not talking about an impossibly high standard of spiritual achievement. Recall that St. Paul tells the Romans, "Ever since the creation of the world [God's] invisible nature, namely, his eternal power and deity, has been clearly perceived in the things that have been made" (Rom. 1:20). Here the apostle speaks to the beginnings of natural contemplation. Abba Evagrius of Pontus (d. 399) says, "As for those who are far from God ... God has made it possible for them to come near to the knowledge of him and his love for them through the medium of creatures."[57] We are not suggesting that anyone become a "mystic" in the sense that this word has acquired in the West. Rather, we are suggesting that some loving attention to the world, particularly in one's own home, family, and line of work, seen dispassionately in the light of the Risen Christ, can be enough to make a beginning. The humblest things are then recognized as more than mere objects. "Regard all the utensils of the monastery and its whole property as if they were the sacred vessels of the altar," *The Rule of St. Benedict* tells us,[58] for indeed, in the light of natural contemplation they are revealed to be so. A person becomes a priest at the altar of his own heart, celebrating that "cosmic liturgy" of which St. Maximus the Confessor speaks. Language, work, art, culture, the humanities, and the natural world too, find their meaning there because the Logos,

> while hiding himself for our benefit in a mysterious way, in the *logoi*, shows Himself to our minds to the extent of our ability to understand, through visible objects which act like letters of the alphabet, whole and complete both

---

[57] Evagrius of Pontus, *Letter to Melania*, also called *The Great Letter*, 6–7, in *Evagrius Ponticus*, A. M. Casiday, Fathers of the Church (NY: Routeledge, 2006), 64.

[58] St. Benedict of Nursia, *The Rule of Saint Benedict*, 31.8, trans. Leonard Doyle (Collegeville, MN: Liturgical Press, 2001), 83.

individually and when related together. He, the undifferentiated, is seen in differentiated things, the simple in the compound. He who has no beginning is seen in things that must have a beginning; the Invisible in the visible; the Intangible in the tangible. Thus He gathers us together in Himself, through every object … enabling us to rise into union with Him, as He was dispersed in coming down to us.[59]

Priest

As we said previously, man is a *microcosm* of the whole created order. His status as a microcosm is in service to his role as a *mediator*, that is, he is called to unify through himself all the various parts of creation. Man is not simply to *be* a microcosm, as an image or icon of the world; rather, he is to *function* as one, to gather into himself all the disparate elements of the created order, material, animal, and spiritual, and to offer them up to God. This is part of the dignity of human persons, their ability to create "events of communion," whereby created things are "liberated from their limitations and are referred to something greater than themselves—to God."[60] It is, in short, the priestly function of mankind. Father Dumitru Stăniloae spoke often

---

[59] St. Maximus the Confessor *Ambigua* (PG 91.1285D-1288A) cited in Olivier Clément, *Roots of Christian Mysticism*, 227–28. The Confessor takes the line, "visible objects which act like letters of the alphabet," from Evagrius of Pontus, *Letter to Melania*, also called *The Great Letter*, 6–7. See Casiday, *Evagrius Ponticus*, Fathers of the Church, 65.

[60] John D. Zizioulas, "Preserving God's Creation: Three Lectures on Theology and Ecology," *King's Theological Review*, 12, no. 1 (1989), 1–5, http://www.resourcesforchristiantheology.org/?p=130#more-130.

of the human person as a "priest of creation."[61] He based his exposition on passages in St. Maximus the Confessor we have already addressed.[62] We briefly summarize Maximus to make the point clearer.

Maximus says that the whole created order was established to celebrate a "cosmic liturgy" and to be transfigured through the priestly mediation of man. This was Adam's task in the beginning, but because of the fall, the priestly function of mediation was corrupted, and Adam was unable to realize his role in the divine plan.[63] Christ, however, by assuming human nature, was himself able to accomplish the cosmic mediation, and each person regenerated in the Church and baptized into Christ is empowered to do the same. Thus, by making progress in the spiritual life, a Christian is able to perceive creation spiritually through natural contemplation, discern the *logoi* hidden in the phenomenal world, and present them as "gifts" to the Lord. As the Orthodox scholar Radu Bordeianu points out, "This attitude toward creation is Eucharistic: humans lift up to God the *logoi* that already belong to him."[64]

In building on the Confessor's thought, Stăniloae develops his notion of mankind as "priests of creation" into a threefold scheme of natural, universal, and ordained priesthood. Because Adam was originally tasked with the role of mediation, of serving a "cosmic liturgy," Stăniloae saw that humanity has a kind

---

[61] See Radu Bordeianu, "Priesthood Natural, Universal and Ordained: Dumitru Stăniloae's Communion Ecclesiology," *Pro Ecclesia* 19, no. 4 (2010): 405–33, esp. 407–17. John Zizioulas makes a point of it, too, in "Preserving God's Creation."

[62] Chiefly, *Mystagogy*, chaps. 3 and 6.

[63] John Zizioulas, "Proprietors or Priests of Creation," 3, identifies Adam's failure to perform his priestly role as "the root of the ecological problem."

[64] Bordeianu, "Priesthood Natural, Universal and Ordained," 407.

of natural priesthood that is inherent in all human beings from the very beginning. It was Adam and Eve's task to exercise this natural priesthood by offering the world that they received from God back to him in thanksgiving. Part of that offering includes the comprehension, shaping, and development of the "unlimited potentiality" in nature, and Stăniloae's thought allows us to see that the natural priesthood extends even to include scientific discovery and its technological applications.[65] Because Orthodox theology teaches that the fall corrupts human nature but does not destroy it, our natural priesthood was certainly impoverished by the fall, but it was not rendered totally ineffective.[66] Given this understanding, Orthodoxy can encourage a positive view of science and technological innovation.

The restoration of the natural priesthood impoverished by the fall is part of the work of Christ. Adam's error was to fail to regard creation as a gift from God and instead see it as an exclusively material reality to be had and used apart from God. However, Christ united the world to God in his assumption of the flesh, and the world became fully transparent to God in him. More than that, through the gift of his sacrifice on the cross, he "restored both the dimension of a gift to the world and our natural priesthood as the capacity to offer creation back to God, especially in the Eucharist. Thus, the human being as priest of creation became able to fully see God's presence in the world

---

[65] See Charles Miller, *The Gift of the World: An Introduction to the Theology of Dumitru Staniloae* (Edinburgh: T&T Clar, 2000), 60–61, cited in Radu Bordeianu, "Priesthood Natural, Universal and Ordained," 408.

[66] Radu Bordeianu, "Priesthood Natural, Universal and Ordained," 408n15, points out that in other of his writings, "Stăniloae explicitly argued against the idea that natural priesthood is ineffectual."

and, by having a Eucharistic attitude toward the universe, to reestablish creation's movement in God and toward God."[67]

The natural priesthood common to all humanity finds its fulfillment in Stăniloae's second category: the universal priesthood of all Christian believers. As creation has become transparent to God through Christ, so we who are baptized into Christ have the capacity to see the transparency of creation, too. We can perceive its spiritual dimension (its *logoi*), and thus see creation as a mystery/sacrament, a visible sign and means for the communication of God's grace. It is the responsibility of the universal priesthood of all Christians to recognize the world as a sacrament, to spiritualize the world and offer it as a gift to God in a cosmic liturgy, but also to take the gift offered to God back into the world, to the rest of mankind and creation,

---

[67] Radu Bordeianu, "Priesthood Natural, Universal and Ordained," 408–9. These themes recall the sacramental theology of the late Fr. Alexander Schmemann (d. 1983), who wrote, *à propos* of our subject,

> The fall of man is the rejection by him of his priestly calling, his refusal to be priest. The original sin consists in man's choice of a non-priestly relationship with God and the world. And perhaps no word better expresses the essence of this new, fallen, non-priestly way of life than the one which in our time has had an amazingly successful career, has truly become the symbol of our culture. It is the word *consumer*. After having glorified himself as *homo faber*, and then *as homo sapiens*, man seems to have found his ultimate vocation as "consumer".... But the truth is, of course, that the "consumer" was not born in the twentieth century. The first consumer was Adam himself. He chose not to be priest but to approach the world as consumer: to "eat" of it, to use and to dominate it for himself, to benefit from it but not to offer, not to sacrifice, not to have it for God and in God.

Alexander Schmemann, *Of Water and the Spirit* (Crestwood, NY: St. Vladimir's Seminary Press, 1974), 96.

and thus transform them into an image of divine communion. Bordeianu says,

> It is important to note that natural priesthood encompasses all human beings. And yet, Christians who share in the sacramental life of the church partake fully in the sacramentality of creation, while non-Christians enjoy it to a lesser degree, since they cannot see the connection between the material world and its salvation in Christ. This distinction in degree, however, does not deny the natural priesthood of non-Christians. Thus, Stăniloae's theology of natural priesthood is relevant for both ecological concerns and interreligious dialogue, since it calls for a common, priestly, and Eucharistic attitude toward creation, an attitude that can, and urgently needs to, be shared among all people, regardless of their religious affiliation.[68]

As the Armenian theologian Vigen Guroian observes, "At the center of the ecological problem is the fact that the original blessing has turned to curse. Only humanity's willing embrace of its priestly and eucharistic vocation will remedy the deep ontological disharmony of the created order."[69] To see how the vocation of "priests of creation" works in restoring creation and offering it to God, we can take for an example the Blessing of Water that is performed as part of the Orthodox Service of baptism.

Before a baptism takes place in the Orthodox Church, the vessel of water is first exorcised and blessed. In exorcising the water, the priest acknowledges its fallen character. He reverses the curse laid on the waters at the fall and undoes the sign of

---

[68] Radu Bordeianu, "Priesthood Natural, Universal and Ordained," 410.

[69] Vigen Guroian, "Ecological Ethics," 161.

destruction and chaos that water had become during the flood in the days of Noah (Gen. 6–7). The priest says in part,

> We pray You, O God, that every aerial and obscure phantom withdraw itself from us; and that no demon of darkness may conceal itself in this water; and that no evil spirit which instills darkening of intentions and rebelliousness of thought may descend into it with him/her who is about to be baptized.

Making the sign of the cross in the water with a hand cross, the priest says three times,

> Let all adverse powers be crushed beneath the image of the sign of the Cross.

Once the exorcism is accomplished and the water is rescued from its fallen state, it is possible for it to be blessed and become a blessing for the one to be baptized in it, becoming

> the water of redemption, the water of sanctification, the purification of flesh and spirit, the loosing of bonds, the remission of sins, the illumination of the soul, the laver of regeneration, the renewal of the Spirit, the gift of adoption to sonship, the garment of incorruption, the fountain of life.

In this way, the nature of the water in the font is restored to its original condition and it becomes "good," as it was in the beginning when God created it. Just as the Holy Spirit hovered over the water "in the beginning" and descended upon Christ at his baptism by John (see Gen. 1:2; Matt. 3:16), so, too, the Holy Spirit descends upon the baptismal waters:

> You hallowed the streams of Jordan, sending down upon them from heaven Your Holy Spirit, and crushed the heads of the dragons who lurked there.

Thus the water of baptism becomes a mystery, a sacrament: a material thing taken from the world, but set apart by man, cleansed, renewed, offered to God, and becomes life-bearing to those who share in it.[70]

A similar thing happens in the Great Blessing of Water, which takes place annually on the Feast of Theophany (January 6): Water is again set apart, exorcised and blessed, with the cross being plunged into the water thrice while the hymn of Theophany is sung. This water is drunk by the faithful and sprinkled throughout the temple and on everyone present so that they can share in "blessing of Jordan" and the renewal of creation that it effects. Furthermore, this holy water is taken home by the faithful, for drinking and blessing throughout the year, and priests visit the homes of their faithful, blessing their houses with it. In this way, the re-creation of the world that is celebrated inside the Church is taken outside the Church, into the world, in fulfillment of the Church's cosmic mission to sanctify the whole world.

According to Zizioulas,

> The priest is the one who freely and, as himself an organic part of it, takes the world in his hands to refer it to God, and who, in return, brings God's blessing to what he refers to God. Through this act, creation is brought into communion with God himself. This is the essence of priesthood, and it is only the human being who can do it, namely, unite the world in his hands in order to refer it to God, so that it can be united with God and thus

---

[70] See Vigen Guroian, "Ecological Ethics," 163–64. Also, on the cosmic aspect of blessing the water of baptism, Bishop Ireneos (Pop), "Orthodox Liturgy and the Care for Creation," in *The Orthodoxy and Ecology Resource Book*, ed. Alexander Belopopsky and Dimitri Oikonomou (Bialystok, Poland: Orthdruk Printing House, 1996), http://www.goarch.org/ourfaith/ourfaith8048/.

> saved and fulfilled. This is so because, as we said earlier,
> only the human being is united with creation while being
> able to transcend it through freedom.[71]

This priestly role that Christ fulfilled through his passion, death, and resurrection has been assigned to his body, the Church. Then the Church, primarily but not exclusively, fulfills this cosmic liturgy through the sacraments (or "mysteries," as the Orthodox prefer to call them).

The principal mystery of the Church, the Eucharist, is celebrated in the Divine Liturgy. In the Byzantine Rite of the Orthodox Church, the central focus of the eucharistic part of the Divine Liturgy is not on the consecration of the bread and wine (either at the "words of institution" or at the *epiklesis*, the calling down of the Spirit on the gifts), nor on the remembrance (*anamnesis*) of the Last Supper or the sacrifice of Christ on the cross; rather, it is on the lifting up of the gifts to God the Father, which is called the *anaphora* (Greek for "lifting up"). Here we see most clearly the liturgical act of offering back to God his own creation in the form of bread and wine. In this way we take what is *good*, the fruit of the earth—wheat and grapes—and through human agency and skill transform them into something *better*—bread and wine—and then offer them to God and receive in return what is *best*: the life-bearing body and blood of Christ. Here we have a paradigm of Orthodox environmental action.[72]

---

[71] John Zizioulas, "Proprietors or Priests of Creation," 3.

[72] Compare Patriarch Bartholomew I (address at the Environmental Symposium, Saint Barbara Greek Orthodox Church, Santa Barbara, CA, November 8, 1997), "our sin toward the world, or the spiritual root of all our pollution, lies in our refusal to view life and the world as a sacrament of thanksgiving, and as a gift of constant communion with God on a global scale," http://www.patriarchate. org/documents/santa-barbara-symposium.

To go further, the meaning of "lifting up" the gifts is even more dramatically shown, because while the deacon elevates the gifts in the *anaphora*, the priest, acting *in persona Christi*, cries aloud, "Your own of Your own we offer unto You, in behalf of all, and for all." In this way, the Church acknowledges that the whole creation belongs to God and offers it all back to him in an act of thanksgiving. (In so doing, the Church reverses the sinful attitude of Adam, who did not offer the world to God, but took it and referred it to himself.)[73] God, having received the offering of his people, and blessed it through the descent of the Holy Spirit on the gifts at the request of the priest in the *epiklesis*, then returns their offering to the faithful. This is marked in the Liturgy when the priest, speaking on behalf of God, exclaims to the people, "The Holy Things are for the holy." There follows immediately the preparation of the gifts for distribution in Holy Communion.

Of course, the Eucharist is communicated to all the faithful present, but the eucharistic liturgy is seen more broadly as the cosmic liturgy because, while the transformation of the holy gifts is exclusively for human consumption and the sanctification of persons, the Divine Liturgy as a whole serves more than human needs. This is so because, as we have seen, mankind is not a part of nature but rather the other way around: Nature is a part of mankind, and when we are bidden by the priest in the Divine Liturgy to "lift up our hearts," and we respond, "we lift them up unto the Lord," we lift up not only our hearts but everything contained in them, which includes not only everyone known to us, but also the whole natural order which we embody as microcosms. Thus the *anaphora* of the Liturgy is not only the lifting up of the cosmos in the bread and wine of the Eucharist, but it is also the lifting up of the cosmos in every human heart

---

[73] John Zizioulas, "Proprietors or Priests of Creation," 3.

which is joined together with the eucharistic offering, making one great offering "in behalf of all, and for all."

In this way the two dimensions of living in the creation that we detailed above, the ascetical and ecclesial dimensions, come together in one moment to serve the recreation and healing of the world.

The ascetical dimension is brought to bear when individual Christians, through asceticism and the practice of virtue (1) advance in the spiritual life, (2) begin through natural contemplation to perceive (in the *logoi*) what God intended for the world to be, (3) realize their role as microcosms and mediators embodying the whole creation, and (4) begin to act toward nature according to the grace afforded to them.

The ecclesial dimension is manifest when individual Christians (1) come together in the Church; (2) recognize their corporate identity as members of the one body of Christ, thus constituting the Church itself as a microcosm and mediator for the world; (3) lift up their hearts to the Lord along with everyone and everything contained in their hearts; (4) unite their hearts with the uplifted gifts of bread and wine in a single offering to God; and (5) share in the transfiguring grace of God when the Holy Spirit is poured out.[74] This last point, that the hearts of all the faithful share in the pouring out of the Holy Spirit, is shown explicitly in the Divine Liturgy at the *epiclesis*, the "calling down" of the Spirit upon the gifts of bread and wine, for the priest does not pray only for the transfiguration of the holy gifts set forth on the altar but for everyone present when

---

[74] They do so according to the logic of the Council of Chalcedon with "no confusion, no change, no division, and no separation" among the assembled faithful or among the elements of creation of which the faithful are microcosms.

he prays, "send down Your Holy Spirit *upon us* and upon these gifts set forth, and make this bread," and so forth.[75]

Thus, through liturgical action human persons serving as "priests of creation" recreate and elevate the whole natural order so that all of nature can (1) be restored to that primordial goodness that God intended it to have, (2) acquire a depth of meaning that it otherwise would not attain (through recognition of its *logoi*), (3) be treated with the reverence due to everything that belongs to God, (4) be freed from its natural limitations (because it is handled according to its true potential intended by God, as seen in the *logoi*), and (5) be united to God through Christ, who is "all, and in all" (Col. 3:11). Having accomplished all of this, the natural order transfigured by grace can be received back into our hands and used for human flourishing in ways not previously realized, for what had previously been corrupted has now become life-bearing. Again, all of this potential is realized when human persons act freely according to the image of God in themselves and offer to God his own of his own, "on behalf of all, and for all."

This point brings us back to Vladimir Solovyov, with whom we began, who said more than a century ago,

> To cultivate the ground means not to misuse, exhaust, or devastate it, but to improve it, to bring it to greater power and fullness of being.… [Nature's] subordinate position in relation to the Deity and humanity does not render it rightless: it has a right to our help in transforming it and uplifting it. Things are rightless, but nature or earth is not merely a thing but an objectified essence, which we can and therefore must help to become spiritualized. The end of labor, so far as material nature is concerned, is not to

---

[75] We feel the text of the Divine Liturgy bears this interpretation, but we hold our opinion lightly and defer to more competent authority if we are shown to be too bold.

> make it an instrument for obtaining things and money, but to perfect it—to revive the lifeless, to spiritualize the material in it.... *Without loving nature for its own sake it is impossible to organize material life in a moral way.*[76]

Thus nature has a right to be transformed and uplifted, spiritualized and revived, and mankind has an obligation to serve that right, to love nature, not for our sake alone, but for its own sake, and not just for the utility that it can provide. We do that when we realize that nature is not merely a thing but a part of our very selves, as we said above. Such a realization requires of us an attitude toward the natural world that does not preclude stewardship of the world and its resources to meet human needs but goes beyond it to the fulfillment and perfection of creation for its own sake.

---

[76] Vladimir Solovyov, *The Justification of the Good*, 299–300. Emphasis in the original.

About the Authors

The Very Reverend Michael Butler is an independent scholar and an archpriest of the Orthodox Church in America and is serving a parish in Olmsted Falls, Ohio. He received his PhD in church history and patristics from Fordham University and his MA in theology and BA in psychology from the University of Dallas.

Andrew Morriss is D. Paul Jones, Jr., and Charlene A. Jones Chairholder in law and professor of business at the University of Alabama in Tuscaloosa. He received his PhD in economics from MIT, his JD and MPA from the University of Texas in Austin, and his AB from Princeton University. He has written extensively on environmental issues.